Victorious Living in a Problematic World

The Divine Design

Revised Edition

David F. Van Hoose

FWB
Publications
The Best is Less

For Worthwhile Books
Columbus, Ohio

TABLE OF CONTENTS

Chapter 4   37-53
The Blessings of God and Major Keys to His Blessings
- A. Four categories of blessings
    1. God blessing People
    2. People blessing God
    3. People blessing people
    4. God and people blessing things
- B. God's blessings and the sources from which they come
    1. Providential acts of God working for us – not against us
    2. Plan of redemption—and all the benefits that pertain to it
    3. Purpose for which we were designed
    4. Prayers offered and answered
    5. Peace of God within
    6. Principles and laws of God, if obeyed, will bring positive results in life
    7. Power of God at work within us
    8. Provisions of God extended to us in time of need
    9. Promises of God claimed by faith
    10. Protection of God around and over us
    11. Personal gifts bestowed upon us
    12. People brought into our life
- C. The major keys to God's blessings
    1. Fear of God
    2. Faith
    3. Humility
    4. Alive in Christ
    5. Infilling of the Spirit and Heart Purity
    6. Biblical thinking
    7. Obedience to the laws, commandments, and principles of God's Word
    8. Acknowledgement of God in all our ways
    9. Delight in the Lord
    10. Generosity
    11. Prayer
    12. Forgiveness

Chapter 5   55-63
The Biblical Lifestyle and Characteristics that Complement our Essential Spiritual Virtues and Honors God's Blessings upon Us
- A. Matthew 5:3-12
- B. Romans 12:9-21
- C. I Corinthians 13:1-8
- D. Galatians 5:13-26
- E. Ephesians 4:25-32, 5:1-5
- F. Philippians 4:4-9, 11, 13, 19
- G. Colossians 3:1-17
- H. I Thessalonians 5:16-24
- I. II Peter 1:4-8

Foreword

Dr. David F. Van Hoose is an educator, administrator, pastor, pastoral counselor and has been my friend for nearly 60 years. It is my esteemed privilege to commend this book to your reading. I know of no one more qualified to write on the subject of living victoriously in these very chaotic days. He uses God's Word rather than human philosophy for his standard of measurement. He recognizes that man is a God-created free and responsible moral being who has a capacity for God and holiness and for high rational thinking and moral choosing wrapped up within his personality.

His concern is that we Christians properly delineate the difference between purity of heart and the maturity of life. It is the premise of this book that the experiences of conversion and sanctification deal with the sin problem in the human life but does not remove any of man's basic humanity. But he reveals that as the result of Adam's fall in the Garden, the human nature has been greatly impaired and is very infirm. Therefore, each of us have our personal psychological baggage not in itself sinful but is in need of constant discipline. Following the promises of God that are listed in II Corinthians 6:14-18, Paul gives instructions for the Christian to follow, *"Having therefore these promises, dearly beloved, let us cleanse ourselves from all filthiness of the flesh and spirit, perfecting holiness in the fear of God."* This book is written to aid the Christian in fulfilling these instructions. I highly recommend this book as a cogent study guide to all serious-minded Christians who would live victorious here and be triumphant hereafter.

--Dr. Nelson S. Perdue, Tenured Evangelist
Church of the Nazarene

Acknowledgements

Special acknowledgement is to be given to the congregation of the Urbana, Ohio Church of Christ in Christian Union. It was through their love and prayers, along with the ministry of Pastor Carl Ogden, that as a teenager I was remarkably converted, and brought into the Kingdom of God.

I will also be forever grateful for the many opportunities the Church afforded me to serve in its local ministries.

Sincere thanks are in order for the many outstanding teachers, who so graciously shared their knowledge and counsel within the classrooms of my formal training.

I am also indebted to the various places of Christian service throughout my ministry. Every opportunity provided wonderful friendships, learning, and personal enrichment.

Finally, a special thanks to my wife, Esther, and our two sons, Tim and Terry. Their ongoing support and loyalty is beyond measure. Words are inadequate to express my gratitude for Esther's selfless spirit, love, prayers, encouragement, and help throughout my ministry. I am especially indebted for her many hours invested in typing and providing editorial assistance in making this book a reality. Also, I would be remiss if I failed to acknowledge, with great appreciation, the editorial review rendered by Shannon Bryant, a great teacher, artist, wife and mother.

Above all, I give thanks to God, whom I acknowledge as the One who has made all things possible through His grace and Divine Providence. Pro 3:5-6

Introduction

The gift of life is given to us for a purpose. God desires to place His blessing upon it, that we, in turn, may fulfill His will, bless others, and be victors and not victims in this problematic world.

But, the curse of sin and evil forces are constant challenges to the "ideal" life God designed for His people.

However, through God's wisdom and mercies, He provided all the moral principles and spiritual resources necessary for His followers to live a fruitful and triumphant life in Christ.

The content contained in this book is presented for the purpose of providing the reader greater insights into:

Life's realities we must confront
God's blueprint by which we were designed
Spiritual virtues by which we are to live for optimal living
The essential keys to God's blessings
The major negative moral forces which contribute to life's problems
The Christian's spiritual resources for victorious living.

It is also to be noted that this book is structured for the purpose of both individual and group study. The reader is encouraged to do further research of the scriptures and subjects presented.

Remember, God did not call us to be:

Victims, but rather, victors
"Overcomed," but rather, overcomers
Losers, but rather, winners
Weak, but rather, strong
Fearful, but rather, courageous
Barren, but rather, fruitful
Cursed, but rather, blessed
Defeated, but rather, delivered.

May the Lord prosper and enrich your spiritual journey and life through His Word and the insights presented in this book.

Chapter 1

Some Major Insights About Life

Our life is a divine masterpiece of creation. *Eph 2:10.* The Psalmist addressed this reality when he wrote "I am fearfully and wonderfully made…" *Ps 139:14.* God planned that our life would flourish with His blessings, and be fruitful, and enjoyable. He desired that we should so live as to enrich the lives of others, bring glory to His name *(Ps 34:1),* and forever be a vital part of His Eternal Kingdom.

However, God's plan was greatly hindered through Adam and Eve's transgression of His one law of prohibition in the Garden of Eden. *Gen 3; Rom 5:12-21.* The curse of sin is the consequence of this one transgression which has had a negative and ricocheting effect upon all the earth and mankind.

Consequently, all creation suffers from its effect. We thus live in a very troubled and problematic world. We are continuously involved in a cosmic battle of evil forces and conflict. However, because of God's love and mercy, He has given us another chance by providing a Plan of Redemption for this world and all who live in it. This Plan of Redemption includes all the spiritual promises and moral laws necessary for Godly living, as revealed in the Scriptures. It includes God's intervention on our behalf, by sending Christ into this world to be our Example, our Sacrifice for sin, and our Redeemer and Savior to cleanse us from all sin.

God sent His Holy Spirit on the Day of Pentecost *(Acts 2:1-4)* to dwell within us, to give us gifts, and empower our lives that we might be victorious over sin in this complex and problematic world. *Rom 8:31; I Jn 4:4, 5:4.*

Anyone who by faith elects to accept Christ as Lord and Savior, and live by God's revealed moral laws and principles, is well on their way toward the restoration of their life and God's Masterpiece. Our total restoration will be finalized on the day of the resurrection of the dead in Christ and the rapture of the living saints of God. *Rom 8:18; I Cor 15:51-55; II Cor 4:17, I Thess 4:16-18; Phil 3:20-21.* But until the day of total redemption, it is wise to keep in perspective the following insights about life.

    A. Life Comes as a Unique Masterpiece from God
       Ps 139:13-18; Jer 1:5, 29:11; Eph 2:10; Phil 2:13

       We are created with uniqueness:
           Gifted uniquely for a purpose and mission in life
           Awesome in uniqueness for there is no one else just like us—unique
               DNA
               Eyes
               Fingerprints
               Gifts
               Hands
               Hair
               Laugh
               Teeth
               Voice, etc.

Miraculous – Your life has been spared by God from death for a specific purpose. Think of the numerous "close calls" life has presented.
Eternity built within – Designed to live forever - *Ecc 3:11 NIV*
Somebody special with special identity with God and with others
Six-Dimensional in our being representing:

      A Physical Dimension – *Rom 12:1; I Cor 3:16, 9:27; II Cor 4:7-8*
      An Intellectual (Mental) Dimension – *Isa 26:3; II Cor 10:5; Col 3:2; Phil 4:8*
      An Emotional Dimension – *Mt 5:4; Eph 4:26, 31*
      A Social Dimension – Mt 5:9, 23-24; Rom 12:18; Heb 12:14
      A Spiritual Dimension – *Jn 4:24; I Thess 5:23*
           (Heart = Soul/Spirit) – *Pro 4:23, 23:7; Mt 5:8, 15:18-19; Acts 15:9; I Tim 1:5*
      A Volitional Dimension – *Gen 2:16-17; Deut 30:19; Josh 24:15; Jn 3:16; Rev 3:20*

Each of these dimensions is inner-connected. If there is dysfunction within any one, it can impact the well-being of any or all of the other dimensions.

Therefore, this gift of life is not to be neglected in any of its dimensions. Each dimension is to be viewed with great respect, and brought under the control of the Spirit, the Word of God, and personal discipline. The Bible teaches that life is to be taken seriously, and we are never to forget how:

      Brief, *Ps 90:10-12*- Average life span is about 28,500 days, and is a temporary assignment here on earth.
      Uncertain, *Jms 4:13-15*
      Fragile,
      Significant, *Jn 3:16*
      Sacred, and
      Eternal it is. *Mk 8:36-37* - Christians are being prepared to live in another world.

B. Life comes with the need for a <u>purpose</u> for which to live, especially a purpose and cause greater than one's self. Everyone is driven by something. What drives you? Faith, fears, family, friends, money, possessions, power, pleasure, popularity, or one or more of these aspects of life?

Life without purpose is a life without meaning. The Bible reveals that God has a specific purpose for each of us. *Jer 1:5, 29:11; Eph 1:1, 2:10; Phil 2:13.* Always remember each person has been given a temporary assignment here on earth.

Living the life for which we were designed, and for the purpose and cause greater than ourselves, will be rewarded with great meaning and fulfillment. Rick Warren, in his book, <u>The Purpose Driven Life</u> amplifies this concept.

The purpose for which we were designed will always be in keeping with our unique gifts, and our deepest God-given inner desire. *Ps 37:4*

C. Life comes with the ability to make choices, the ability of others to make choices which may impact our life, and also the inability to make some choices.
Choices impact every aspect of our life. Some choices are our choices. Some choices are the choices of others, and choices always bring about consequences.
Choices made without a moral compass, and the lack of good judgment, will ultimately result in some form of injury, either to self, others, or both.

Finally, our ability to make some choices is greatly restricted. Much of our life centers around the choices and circumstances of which we had no control. For example, we did not choose:

> our gender or race
> our limitations
> our abilities
> our birth place/nation
> our siblings
> our parents, etc.

Most of our personal choices are moral choices, for we are moral beings.
Every person is confronted with the reality of being involved in a moral universe and a "cosmic" battle. Christians are caught between two kingdoms: the Kingdom of Darkness and the Kingdom of Heaven. Each day multiple moral choices must be made, such as:

> Authenticity vs hypocrisy
> Biblical thinking vs secular thinking
> Commitment vs broken promises
> Disciplined vs undisciplined
> Emotional/spiritual cleansing vs emotional and spiritual garbage
> Faith vs doubt
> Generosity vs greed
> Hope vs despair
> Investment vs squandering
> Joy vs lament
> Kindness vs harshness
> Love vs hate
> Mercy vs unforgiveness
> Obedience vs disobedience
> Optimism vs pessimism
> Praise vs complaint
> Prayer vs worry
> Spirit vs flesh
> Truth vs deception
> Victory vs defeat and surrender

A careful study of *Ephesians 4:25-5:5* reveals the reality of moral choices with which we are constantly confronted. Each day Christians are required to make choices of moral integrity and godliness.

D. Life comes with constant changes, and with changes comes the potential of both gains and losses.
Think of the changes that have come into your life because of:

> Development of technology
> Disease
> Disabilities
> Death
> Relationships (deceased, alienated, broken, relocated, etc.)
> Aging
> Weather
> Cycle of life
> Governmental laws and regulations
> Problems

We have a natural desire for elements of permanence and stability. Conversely, there are times when change is necessary and even anticipated. But the fact remains that change will always bring forms of loss, stress, and needed adjustments. Consequently, people by and large struggle with change. Take time to reflect on the many losses that change has brought into your life. Ponder the thought that "aging" is a series of ongoing losses in life, and with loses comes forms of grief.

E. Life comes with its own judicial system – the conscience and God's perfect judgment. Conscience is that inner voice that either condemns with guilt or exonerates with peace.

Conscience is not always a true judge or guide. Some people are troubled with an overly sensitive conscience. Others appear to have no sense of conscience. They are known as "sociopathic personalities" who are capable of committing horrendous crimes without guilt. It is vitally important that our conscience be permitted to function as it was designed, for we can never have true inner harmony without a "good" conscience. *I Tim 1:5*

F. Life comes with personal responsibility.
Unless impaired by injury, disease, mental incompetency, or infancy, we are responsible for the:
> Words we speak
> Thoughts we entertain
> Reactions and responses we give to life's adversities
> Attitudes we exude
> Choices we make
> Kind of person we are and will become
> Kinds of friendships with whom we align ourselves
> Stewardship, or lack thereof, of our time, talent, treasures, responsibilities, body, mind, emotions, social, spiritual, vocational, and financial life.
> Spiritual legacy we leave behind and the spiritual destiny to which we will go.

Our spiritual health and quality of life will always demand personal responsibility and accountability.

G. Life demands that we live with our own inner self.
Each person must live with their:
> Failures and regrets
> Feelings
> Thoughts
> Inner and outer honesty
> Memories
> Motives
> Needs
> Beliefs
> Values
> Priorities
> Purpose for life
> Goals or lack thereof
> Relationships
> Reactions and responses to life's challenges
> Attitudes
> Changes in life

Choices
Conscience
Investments in life, or lack thereof
Emotions
Self-focus, respect, and image
Seasonal clock (chapters of life)
Spiritual journey and immortality
Weaknesses and Strengths
Words spoken

H. Life demands that we deal with our own failures and regrets.
Life is filled with forms of "failure." Our body, mind, emotions, social, spiritual, and vocational life is always confronted with the possibility of failure. Healthy living requires a fair and appropriate response to life's failures. We can choose to dwell on them or release them. We can make our failures or regrets one of 2 stones; a stepping stone or a stumbling block.

If the body fails, we have the option of medical care and perhaps a healthier lifestyle.

If our mind fails, we have the option of seeking why it failed or accepting it as a part of our life's limitations.

If our emotions fail, we have the option of personal evaluation and spiritual and professional care.

If our social life has failed, we have the option of correction, reconciliation, forgiveness, learning greater social skills, etc.

If our spiritual life has failed, we have the option of confession and correction.

If our vocational life has been a failure, we have the option of learning from it and making necessary adjustments for future success.

Failures and regrets are a part of this problematic world. But God, in His wisdom, can take life's failures and regrets and convert them into the refining of our character. He can teach us some of life's greatest lessons, and use them to demonstrate His power within and through us, and to bring glory to His Name. *Jms 1:2-5*

I. Life demands that we deal with life's adversities and offenses, and our own unique set of problems.
There are problems common to all, and problems that are unique to each individual. We all must adjust to our losses, changes, making "right" decisions, managing our health, maintaining meaningful relationships, etc. But there is also the reality that each person will experience their own unique combination of problems unlike that of others. Name the major problems with which you are currently dealing.

The way we respond will forever be etched within our mind and the minds of those who observe us. The Christian's response is to reflect a quality of character that adds credibility to our faith while bringing honor to God and the Gospel we embrace. Natural responses are greatly influenced by our maturity level, environmental background, thinking style, temperament, and physiology. Biblical insights and Christian maturity will enable a Christian to respond to life's problems in a healthier and more victorious way.

J. Life constantly confronts us with our own mortality.
The death of others is a reminder of the mortality of life. Each day the well-being of our life
is exposed to various threats. There are also specific moments in which we are made to
think, "This may be the end."

Pause for a moment and reflect on the many life threatening situations you have
encountered. These moments present themselves in the form of:
> Accidents
> "Close calls"
> Diseases
> Environmental threats
>> Storms
>> Earthquakes
>> Floods
>> Lightning strikes
>> Criminal activity, etc.

For some reason your life has been spared while the lives of others were not. Remember
the words recorded in the Book of Lamentations, *"It is of the Lord's mercies (love) that we
are not consumed, because his compassions fail not. They are new every morning: great
is thy faithfulness." Lam 3:22-23*

Never take life for granted. Give thanks to Almighty God and endeavor to fulfill the purpose
for which you were designed.

K. Life is not always fair, just, or pleasant. Everyone has felt hurt, rejected, or given an unfair
blow in life. Some more than others. Sometimes bad things come to good people. Joseph
was a godly and just young man, but became a victim of his brother's jealousies who sold
him into slavery. He was a morally pure young man, but was falsely accused by Potipher's
seductive wife, and was thus cast into prison.

Job was a man whom the Bible says was, *"…blameless and upright; he feared God and
shunned evil." NIV Because* of his integrity, God blessed him mightily. However, Satan
falsely accused him as one who served God because of God's blessing upon him.
Consequently, he was put to the test. Through this cosmic conflict he lost his health,
wealth, children, and was falsely accused by his three "friends."

Paul was the called Apostle of God, yet was treated unfairly and unjustly. Life was tough
and brought him much suffering for the cause of Christ.

But God keeps the record, and ultimately the righteous are vindicated, if not in this life, in
the life to come. Until then, we are to maintain Biblical thinking and strong faith in God's
providence, promises, and provisions. We must never allow our attitude to become trapped
in negativity, resentfulness, or bitterness toward life.

L. Life comes with the reality that we will treat God, spiritual life, self, others, and the things
around us (possessions, philosophies, powers, institutions, etc.) according to the value we
place on each. Priorities come out of values and out of priorities and values come our level
of commitment and the goals we pursue.

M. Life comes with the reality that we will always move in a particular direction as determined by the:

> Choices we and others make
> Words we speak
> Faith we exercise
> Attitudes we exude
> Investments we make – *Gal 6:7*
> Thoughts we think
> Heart quality we possess – *Pr 23:7*
> Hopes we entertain
> People with whom we closely associate
> Purpose for which we live
> Goals set and commitments we honor
> Circumstances of which we have no control

N. Life comes with God's specific blueprint by which we are designed for optimal living. God's blueprint requires essential spiritual virtues by which we are to live. Greater detail is given to this subject in Chapter 2 entitled, "The Basic Spiritual Blueprint by Which We Were Designed to Live."

Review these insights and reflect on those that stand out in your mind. Briefly describe why you think they are especially meaningful to you.

Chapter 2

The Basic Spiritual Blueprint by Which We Were Designed to Live

God designed our life to be lived by a basic spiritual blueprint that is to be governed by moral laws and spiritual principles. Those who comply with God's design will be rewarded with a life of purpose, blessing, meaning, fulfillment, and an inner sense of personal well-being.

The Bible reveals that God designed us to live our life:

A. To the fullest within the boundaries of Biblical truth. *Ps 16:11, 23:4-6, 32:11, 40:1-3, 100:4; Isa 58:11; Jn 7:38, 10:10, 15:11*

Living life to the fullest is a life:
--Alive in Christ – II Cor 5:17; Col 3:11; Jn 3:1-7
--Filled with the Spirit – *Acts 4:31; Eph 5:18 E.g. The Day of Pentecost – Acts 2:1-4*
--Of obedience to God's moral laws – *Deut 11:26-27; Josh 1:8; Ps 1:1-3*
--Connected by faith with God's
      Providence – *Rom 8:28*
      Plan of Redemption – Jn 3:16; Rom 5:1
      Purposes – *Jer 1:5, 29:11*
      Prayer Benefits – *Jer 33:3; Jms 5:16*
      Peace – *Phil 4:6-7*
      Principles – *Eph 4:25-32, 5:1-5; I Thess 5:16-23*
      Power – *Acts 1:8; Eph 3:20*
      Provisions – *Phil 4:19*
      Promises – *Rom 15:4; II Pt 1:4*
      Protection – Ps 34:7; Isa 54:17
      Preparation for our eternal existence – *Jn 11:25, 14:1-3; Rom 8:18; II Cor 4:17; Phil 3:20-21; Rev 21:4*
      People – *Heb 10:25; Jms 5:16*
--Out of which comes spiritual
      Love beyond measure
      "Joy unspeakable and full of glory"
      "Peace that passes all understanding"

Liberty	Faith	Hope
Energy – enthusiasm	Anticipation	Optimism
Abundance	Inspiration	Praise
Fervency	Trust	Expectancy
Satisfaction	Harmony	Sense of well-being.

Remember, God did not design us to live a life of:
      Pessimism and negativity
      Oppression and despair
      Worry, fear and anxiety
      Envy
      Resentment

Always keep this thought before you, "God works within the spiritual realm of the positive, and not the negative."

B. Lovingly in the context of God's love—the greatest moral force in the universe.
Mt 5:43-44; Jn 13:35, 15:12; Rom 12:9-10, 13:8-9; I Cor 13:1-14:1; I Tim 1:5; I Pt 1:22; II Pt 1:6-7; I Jn 4:7-8, 16

III. Stephen, the first Christian martyr, demonstrated this moral force when he said, *"Lay not this sin to their charge." Acts 7:60*

What is the quality and quantity of your Christian love? Does your Christian character allow you to bless, forgive, love, give unto, and pray for your enemies? *Mt 5:43-44; Rom 12:19-21*

C. Abundantly in the context of God's blessings, whereby one's life is increased in:
    Influence for the good
    Contributions toward life
    Effectiveness in living
    Quality and quantity of life
Deut 8:18, 11:26-27, 28, 30:19; II Chron 16:9; Josh 1:8; Ps 1:1-3, 115:13-14; Pro 22:4; Jer 29:11; Jn 10:10, 15:2; II Pt 1:5-8; III John 2

The Bible teaches that we were designed for fruitfulness (*Jn 15:2*), and growth, *(II Pt 1:5-7)* and not for barrenness or stagnation.

D. Triumphantly in the context of God's promises, protection, and spiritual powers. (Refer to Chapter 7).
Duet 20:4, 33:25-27; Josh 1:9; Isa 40:31, 41:10, 54:17, 58:11; Jn 14:27, 16:33; Rom 8:31, 35-39; Phil 1:21, 4:13; I Jn 4:4

Even though we encounter numerous battles, adversities, trials, tests, losses, and enemies in life, we have not been called to be failures, but rather:
    Victors and not victims
    Overcomers and not the "over-comed"
    Winners and not losers
    Strong and not weak
    Courageous and not fearful
    Blessed and not cursed
    Delivered and not defeated.

God's Word clearly states that none need to fail. No matter the attacks that may come, or the struggles we may encounter, we are assured in God's Word that we are not the:
    Abandoned ones
    Beaten down ones
    Cast away ones
    Defeated ones
    Enemy besieged ones, or the
    Forgotten ones.

But rather, we are the servants of the Almighty God, and triumph flows through our total being. God has provided all the resources of Heaven essential for our spiritual success through:

His Son, and the Plan of Redemption
His Spirits' gifts, ministries and empowerment
His Body, the Church, and its ministries, fellowship, and combined faith and prayers
His Word and its principles, His promises, and spiritual insights

Therefore, we have all the necessary resources to live a triumphant and victorious life in a problematic world—a life where in we can:
Maximize our full potential in Christ
Experience an inner sense of harmony and well-being
Achieve a quality and quantity of life that God designed for us
Triumph over all of life's adversities
Advance God's Kingdom within the world around us
Bless others and the world in which we live
Claim God's promises for every day events
Declare the whole counsel of God
Exemplify the grace of God
Fight the good fight of faith
Glorify Christ in all we do
Help others on their journey of life
Inspire all who come across our path, and
Joyfully experience the joy of the Lord within our heart.

However, this kind of life does not come from wishful thinking. We live in a world infested with evil forces and sin's curse (*Gen 3:1-4; Rom 5:12).* It is a world that resists God's Kingdom and all who seek to be a part of it.

Remember, God does not want His people to be problem-centered in a problematic world. Rather, it is His will to teach us how our life can emerge far above our earthly challenges. It is His desire to empower us to live a life that attracts His blessings, favor, and smile. It is His plan to help us to release our problems into His providential care so that He might convert them for our good, and enable us to use them for His glory, and demonstrate a triumphant life in Christ.

E. Harmoniously in the context God's imparted Holiness which brings about:
Purity of Heart – *Ps 24:3-5, 51:10, 139:23-24; Mt 5:8; Acts 15:9; I Tim 1:5; I Pt 1:22*
Peace with God and the pursuit of peace with others – *Mt 5:9; Rom 5:1, 12:18; Heb 12:14*
Attitudes of Christ – humility, obedience, submission, forgiveness, love – *Phil 2:1-5*
Perfection of motive (motivational purity) which brings about authenticity within and without – *Mt 5:48; Eph 4:25; I Pt 2:1-2*
Perfect love –*I Jn 4:17 I Cor 13; Jn 13:35, 15:12*

God has always desired a Holy people. This concept is seen both in the Old and New Testament.

In the Old Testament God desired a:
Holy Nation
Holy Laws
Holy Sabbath
Holy Tabernacle
Holy Altar

Holy Place
Holy of Holies
Holy Sacrifices
Holy Priests

In the New Testament God sent His:
Holy Son, who lived a
Holy Life, and taught
Holy Principles, and became a
Holy Sacrifice, on the Cross, shedding His
Holy Blood, that we might become a
Holy People, and go to a
Holy Heaven, in which there are only
Holy People,
Holy Angels, and a
Holy God.

To become a holy person, a holy heart is required. A holy heart comes only from a holy God, for there is no holiness apart from God. Holiness is the essence of God's true nature. We can never become holy apart from God's impartation of His nature to us. This impartation can only be fully obtained through a New Birth Experience brought about by the convicting and drawings of God's Holy Spirit upon the human heart. Whoever responds to God's convicting power, in the spirit of faith and humility, and a true confession of personal sins to God, will be "born again" within his or her spiritual heart. *Jn 3:1-7* This spiritual experience brings about God's forgiveness of all committed sins. *I Jn 1:9*

God's nature and Spirit is now imparted to our spirit. But for the heart to be totally pure and fully possessed by God's holy nature, there is the need for a deeper cleansing. There is a cleansing by the Blood of Christ to purge the heart from the very *"principle of sin." It is* that inner moral force that propels people to commit acts of sin against God, self, and others.

Total consecration of one's will and life to the Lordship of Christ is essential for a total cleansing of the heart from this "sin principle," sometimes called the "root of sin," This spiritual experience is to be pursued and completed sometime subsequent to the New Birth experience. The sooner the better!

Once experienced the believer is no longer governed by a "carnal" disposition, but rather by the control of a clean heart and total infilling of the Spirit. *I Cor 2:14-3:1-3; Eph 5:15-18*

The reader is encouraged to read <u>A Plain Account of Christian Perfection</u> by John Wesley, Founder of Methodism, for greater insight into this subject. The different Biblical expressions for the *"principle of sin"* are listed in Chapter 4 of this book, <u>Victorious Living in a Problematic World.</u>

F. Joyfully in the context of God's joy through Christ and the Holy Spirit. *Ps 16:11, 32:11, 34:1, 40:1-3, 100:1, 4; Neh 8:10; Jn 15:11; Acts 13:52; Rom 14:17; Gal 5:22; Phil 4:4; I Thess 5:16; I Pt 1:8;*

Spiritual joy and its derivatives is a major theme throughout the Bible. In fact, the New Testament begins with joy on earth and ends with joy in heaven.

The following word study reveals the numerous references to a joyful heart in connection with a powerful and personal relationship with God and His will, way, and word (KJV).

Joy – 218 times
Rejoice or rejoicing – 286 times
Gladness – 47 times
Happy or happiness – 30 times
Praise (NIV) – 363 times
The Book of Philippians refers to joy, rejoice, and gladness – 19 times

Christian joy is not easily understood in this problematic world. For its true meaning must be viewed in a multiphasic manner. It is that which includes:

A spiritual state of mind
An attitude
A behavior
An emotion and
A quality and quantity of an inner sense of well-being.

This inner sense of joy and well-being is derived from a combination of the following:

Relational harmony with God and others as much as possible within one's self
Serving a purpose and cause greater than self
Faith in and prayers to God
Freedom from sin and emotional and spiritual bondage
Authenticity within and without
Attitude of optimism
Infilling of the Spirit – *Eph 5:18; Gal 5:22*
Truth of God's Word within – *Jn 4:24, 8:32, 14:6*
Hope that comes out of faith
God's love and peace
Biblical thinking whereby we are able to:
    Perceive
    Evaluate and
    Interpret life's events in the context of God's:
        Providence
        Plan of Redemption
        Purpose
        Prayer response to our prayers
        Peace
        Principles
        Power
        Promises
        Provision
        Protection
        Preparation for our heavenly home – *Jn 14:1-3*

Joyful Christian living generates spiritual:
Life
Inspiration
Fervency and fire
Excitement – energy

But beware! Christian joy can be stolen by the joy robbers in life! (Refer to Chapter 7, Section 10.) Always guard and protect it, for joy is a powerful source of spiritual strength. *Neh 8:10*

G. Relationally in the context of:
> Communion and fellowship with God in the spirit of worship
> Communion and fellowship with others in the spirit of honor, humility, love, and respect *I Cor 1:9, 3:16; II Cor 6:14-7:1; Lev 26:12; Ez 36:25-27; Mt. 5:9, 23-24, 43-44; Rom 12:9-10, 13-21; Gal 5:13-15, 6:1; Heb 12:14; I Pt 1:22; II Pt 1:7*

We are designed as relational beings with relational needs. We have an innate need for fellowship and communion with an Almighty God. That need is met through confession, worship, prayer, praise, and reading and meditating on God's Holy Scriptures.

Our relational dimension also represents the need for communion and fellowship with others.

The New Testament presents a relational gospel which includes a "one another gospel." There are at least 59 "one another's" in the New Testament –
> 1/3 given to church unity
> 1/3 given to love and respect for "one another"
> 15% centered around the spirit of humility and submission toward "one another"
> 60% written by the Apostle Paul.

Listed below are many of the New Testament "one another's."
> Accept one another – *Rom 15:7*
> Admonish one another – *Col 3:16; Rom 15:14*
>
> Bear with each other – *Col 3:13*
> Bear one another's burdens – *Gal 6:2*
> Build up one another – *I Thess 5:11*
>
> Comfort one another – *I Thess 4:18*
> Confess your sins to one another – *Jms 5:16*
>
> Devoted to one another – *Rom 12:10*
>
> Edify one another – *I Thess 5:11*
> Encourage one another – *Heb 3:13; I Thess 3:12*
>
> Forbear one another – *Eph 4:2; Col 3:13*
> Forgive one another – *Eph 4:32; Col 3:13*
>
> Greet one another – *I Pt 5:14*
>
> Harmony with one another – Rom 12:16
> Honor one another – Rom 12:10
>
> Instruct one another – *Rom 15:14*
>
> Judge not one another – *Rom 14:13*

Kind to one another – *Eph 4:32*

Live in harmony with one another – *Rom 12:16*
Love one another – *Jn 13:34, 35, 15:12, 17; I Jn 3:11, 23, 4:7, 11, 12; II Jn 5*

Patience with one another – *Eph 4:2*
Peace with one another – *Mk 9:50*
Pray for one another – *Jms 5:16*

Serve one another – *Gal 5:13*
Speak to one another – *Eph 5:19*
Spur on one another – *Heb 10:24*
Submit to one another – *Eph 5:21*

Teach one another – *Col 3:16*

Wash one another's feet – *Jn 13:14*

Remember, this powerful spiritual truism: "The quality of your spiritual well-being is highly correlated with the quality of your interpersonal relationships." *Mt 5:23-24, 6:12, 14-15; Mk 11:25-26; Lk 17:3-5; Gal 6:1; Heb 12:14*

H. Prayerfully in the context of faith in God and His promises. *Ps 5:3; Jer 33:3; Hab 2:4; Mt 6:6, 7:7, 11, 9:29, 17:20; Rom 1:17; Gal 3:11; Eph 6:18; Phil 4:6; Col 4:2; I Thess 5:17; I Tim 2:8; Heb 4:14-16, 10:38, 11:6 Jms 5:16*

The practice of spiritual laws of prayer and faith are essential for a godly life. These two themes are paramount in achieving spiritual success with God in this problematic world.

Prayers to God and a faith in God (gods) appear to be universal. They are programmed within the human heart to be developed and exercised on a daily basis. We function best when these two spiritual entities are honored and applied in our life's journey. (Please refer to Chapter 4, paragraph 11 for additional insights into this subject.)

I. Productively in the context of physical and spiritual work. *Gen 2:15; Ex 20:9; Ps 128:2, 138:8; Pro 6:6-8, 12:11, 18:9; Ecc 3:2; Mt 25:14-30; Eph 4:28; I Thess 4:11-12; II Thess 3:10-11*

To work is to honor God's blueprint by which we were designed and will bring a special blessing from God. The Bible teaches two categories of work to be done, and each is to be done to honor and glorify the Lord. *I Cor 10:31; Col 3:17, 23*

Physical work: Contributing to the meeting of physical needs within our physical world and the world around us. *Gen 2:15 states, "The Lord God took the man and put him in the Garden of Eden to work and take care of it."*

Numerous scriptures validate the need for and the value of physical labor – *Ps 90:17; Pro 12:11, 24, 13:4, 14:23; I Tim 5:8; II Tim 2:6*

Spiritual work: Contributing to the spiritual and social transformation of the world and people around us. Christ identified His followers as the *"salt" and "light"* of the world. *(Mt 5:13-14)* Christians are mandated to evangelize, teach, and minister to all who are not a part of the Kingdom of God. *(Mt 28:19-20)* Also, our spiritual labor is to be social in nature by caring for the physically needy and oppressed. *(Mt 25:31-46)*

The Biblical principle of stewardship is to be applied in all we do with the time, talents, and treasures God has entrusted into our hands. Productive work requires good stewardship, and good stewardship will always produce good works.

J. Perpetually in the context of eternal life.
God wills that we prepare for and keep in perspective our eternal existence. This is to be a primary part of our daily living, and the interpretation of life's events. *Jn 3:16, 5:28-29, 11:25, 14:1-3; Rom 8:18; I Cor 2:9, 15:51-55; II Cor 4:17; Phil 3:10-11, 20-21; I Thess 4:16-18; Rev 21:4*

The concept that we were designed with eternity within is clearly stated in *Ecc 3:10, "He (God) has made everything beautiful in its time. He has also set eternity in the hearts of men…" NIV*

Consequently, eternity is a universal concept reflected in all cultures and societies. Those who honor and respect this spiritual reality align themselves with God's blueprint and have taken a major step toward the perpetuity of life.

However, this knowledge must be associated with an inner awareness *"that all have sinned and come short of the glory of God." (Rom 3:23)* It is sin (man's disobedience to God) that has brought eternal death and separation from God. *(Rom 6:23)* But God's love and mercy has provided a "Plan of Redemption" for sin's devastating consequences. This redemptive plan is contained within the Gospel of Christ. It is a gospel that teaches and provides for atonement and cleansing from all sin through Christ's shed blood and sacrificial death on the cross.

Consequently, all who confess Christ as Lord, and confess by faith their sins to Him, receive forgiveness and eternal life. *Jn 3:16; Rom 3:23, 6:23, 10:9-10; I Jn 1:9*

Chapter 3

The Need for a Spiritually Healthy "Heart" and Essential Spiritual Virtues

God's blueprint requires the need for a spiritually healthy heart, and the possession of specific essential spiritual virtues for optimal living.

A. The Spiritual Heart – *II Chron 16:9; Ps 19:14, 24:3-5, 51:10, 139:23-24; Pro 4:23, 23:7; Mt 5:8, 15:19-20, 22:37; Acts 15:9; I Tim 1:5; I Pt 1:22.*

God's blueprint includes the design for a well-orchestrated inner life. The Bible refers to it as our "spiritual heart."

The word "heart" is used metaphorically in the Bible and is referenced numerous times, occurring over 600 times in the Old Testament and 210 times in the New Testament. The extensive use of this word gives credence to its extreme significance in Biblical studies. A thorough study of this subject must include the usage of the various words for the heart found in the original languages in which the Bible was written.

The key Old Testament Hebrew words are *Leb, Lebab* and *Nehesh.* The noun *Leb* and its synonym *Lebab* convey the meaning of man's:
> Personality
> Inner being that is often connected with the soul
> Inner life that controls the center of desires, emotions, will, inclination
> Center of moral life
> Center of mind, memory, knowledge
> Center of conscience
> Center of the "principle of sin" – pride, rebellion, etc.

The Hebrew word *Nehesh* is translated 15 times "heart" in the King James Version and conveys the idea of man's life, soul, or self.

The key New Testament Greek word is *Kardia.* It conveys the meaning of the center of man's:
> Will
> Intellect
> Conscience
> Emotions

Sometimes the original language terms for heart, soul, *(psuche)* and spirit *(pneuma)* overlap, and therefore must be carefully interpreted in the context of the scriptural passage in which they are found.

It is also to be noted that much debate centers around similarities and differences between the "spirit" and the "soul" of man as related to the "heart." (dichotomy vs trichotomy theory).

It is not in the scope of this writing to deal with the many complexities related to this theological debate. But an attempt is made to present a brief and general summation of what is meant by the "heart, spirit, and soul of man."

This definition is based on the above meanings associated with the heart, and many New Testament scriptures, such as: *Jn 4:24; Phil 3:3; Rom 8:10; I Thess 5:23; I Cor 2:14-3:4, 14:14; Heb 4:12.*

The Spiritual HEART is known as the:
Control center of our life – *Pro 4:23*
Container of the "sin principle" with which we were born – *Jer 17:9*
Container of our inner sanctuary wherein God dwells within the righteous –
    I Cor 3:16
Container of our Spirit and Soul.

Spirit (God consciousness) consists of our:
Consciousness of God and the spiritual world
Connectedness to God, the spiritual world, and to one another
Communion with God in worship – *Jn 4:24*
Climate of personality – Every person has a personality *climate, atmosphere* and *temperature.* People quickly detect our personality *climate* and will
perceive our spirit to be:
    Anxious or relaxed
    Bitter or tender
    Cold or warm and friendly
    Critical or complimentary
    Demanding or yielding
    Envious or grateful
    Fearful or peaceful
    Fervent or slothful – *Acts 18:25; Rom 12:11*
    Greedy or benevolent
    Hateful or loving
    Indifferent or compassionate
    Jealous or respectful
    Troubled or composed – *Jn 13:21*
Intuition – Inner knowing (discernment)

The Soul (self-consciousness) is referenced nearly 800 times in scripture and includes our:
Personality
Mind and intellect
Inclinations
Desires
Will
Emotions
Conscience – our judicial system
Connectedness with our spirit and body (world consciousness).

The soul's moral health has tremendous impact upon every aspect of our total being, including our spirit and body. This is reflected in John's words to a faithful believer when he wrote:

"Beloved, I wish above all things that thou mayest prosper and be in health, even as thy soul prospereth." III Jn 2 KJV)

"Beloved, I pray in all respects you may prosper and be in good health, just as your soul prospers." (NASV)

"Beloved, I pray that you may prosper in every way and (that your body) may keep well, even as (I know) your soul keeps well and prospers." (Amp NT)

The above information is provided not only for insight, but also as a spiritual challenge. A challenge to become spiritually introspective, and to evaluate your own quality of inner life and well-being. *Ps 139:23-24*

B. The Essential Spiritual Virtues (Parts) by Which we are Designed for Optimal Living
    God also designed us with the <u>need for special essential spiritual</u> virtues and components necessary for overall well-being, and God's special blessings.

    These essential virtues or components can be compared to the necessary parts of an automobile, human body, clock, or plane. For example:
        an automobile has 1800 basic parts with a total of 30,000 total parts
        the body has 7500 named parts
        a clock has 130 to 300 parts
        a 737 Boeing commercial airliner has 367,000 parts

    For an engine to achieve its maximum power, or a clock to perform at its highest level of precision, all parts must be in place and operate according to design. Any missing part, or malfunction of any part, greatly impedes the overall performance for which it was designed. The same is true for each of us. If our spiritual life is to function at its best, be truly blessed by God, and serve as God's sanctuary within, these essential virtues or components cannot be taken lightly. Therefore, it is incumbent upon us to incorporate and cultivate these special essential virtues, and seek to live a lifestyle that will complement each of them. The more they are incorporated and honored, the greater will be our spiritual health, soul prosperity, and God's blessings upon us.

    Any Christ-centered person who elects to do so, will be rewarded with God's special blessings, and experience a life of optimal spiritual living characterized with:
        Inner harmony,
        Inner sense of fulfillment and meaning,
        Inner sense of spiritual well-being, and an
        Inner and outer quality and quantity of life.

    Failure to do so greatly restricts spiritual well-being, and our journey with God. Upon recognizing the significance of the above spiritual realities, it is important that the following question be addressed:

    What are the Specific Essential Spiritual Virtues by which we are Designed?

The following list of spiritual virtues is provided for personal insight. This list is also presented for a self-evaluation of your own character and spiritual quality of inner life in Christ. It is of special interest to note that while all of the following spiritual virtues are essential for optimal living, some are <u>absolutely essential</u> for any form of spiritual life, such as confession, faith, forgiveness, etc. Others are essential but they are not on the same level. For example, the attitude of optimism, laughter, poise, moderation, etc., are very commendable traits but they are not at the level of required faith, confession, or forgiveness.

On a scale of 1 to 5 (1=poor; 3=average; 5=excellent) subjectively evaluate your spiritual life in the context of the following spiritual and moral components (virtues). Remember, we function best when the following characteristics and virtues are a part of our spiritual life.

____1. **Acknowledgement of God** in all our ways. *Pro 3:5-6; Jn 3:1-7; II Cor 5:17;*
How much do you acknowledge God in your actions, thoughts, speech?

____2. **Attitude of Optimism** which exudes faith, anticipation, inspiration, thanksgiving, hope, praise, expectancy, love, joy, and peace. *Ps 34:1, 100:4; Neh 8:10; Rom 12:12, 15:4; II Cor 6:10; Phil 2:14-15; I Thess 5:16.* Attitude reflects the quality of our "spirit," and determines in part our spiritual altitude.

____3. **Bless** God, people, and life—don't curse it. *Ps 34:1, 103:1-2; Rom 12:14*

____4. **Biblical Thinking** (major components of Biblical thought), *Josh 1:9; Ps 1:1-3, 23:1-6; Pro 4:20-23, 23:7; Isa 26:3; Rom 12:2; Eph 4:23; Col 3:2,10; II Cor 10:5 Phil 4:8.* (Thoughts affect every cell of our body.)

____5. **Confessions**—Christ is Lord; sins, faults, and personal needs. *Rom 10:9-10; Jms 5:16; I Jn 1:9* Confession is good for the soul.

____6. **Commitment and Consecration** to a cause, power, and purpose greater than self, which is Christ and His Kingdom. *Mt 6:33; Lk 9:57-62, 12:16-34; Rom 12:1; Gal 2:20; Phil 1:21, 3:10* What is your level of commitment?

____7. **Deligh**t in the Lord. *Ps 37:4, 145:19* (Pleasure, satisfaction fulfillment), and He will delight in you. *Isa 62:4, 65:18*

____7. **Determination** (will power). *II Cor 2:2; Gal 6:9; Eph 6:10-18; Phil 3:13-14; II Pt 1:5-8*
Life is a battle between many major inner voices and the Kingdoms of Evil and Good.

____9. **Disciplined** Spiritually. *Mt 16:24; I Cor 9:27; Gal 5:16-26; Eph 5:15, 6:10,13; Phil 3:13-14; Col 3:17; II Pt 1:5-8; Ps 5:3* – Discipline over our Holy Habits and the 7 major areas of our life: physical, mental, emotional, social, spiritual, financial, and vocational.

____10. **Emotional and Spiritual Cleansing.** (We were not designed for sin.) *I Jn 1:9; Eph 4:31; Col 3:5-8.*

____11. **Empathy and Sensitivity** toward others. *Rom 12:13, 15; Eph 4:32; Mt 7:16; Ps 41:1-3.*

____12. **Faith** in God and His Word. *Heb 11:6; Hab 2:4; Rom 1:16-17; Gal 3:11; Heb 10:38; Mt 8:13, 9:22, 29, 17:20, 19:26; Lk 1:37; Mk 9:23*

___13. **Fear of the Lord**. *Pro 1:7, 9:10, 14:27, 22:4; Rom 3:18*. Involves Focus – Exaltation – Awe/Wonder – Respect and Reverence for His Name, Nature, Will, Way, Word, and Wrath (used 147 times in the Bible).

___14. **Forgiveness**. *Mt 6:12; Mk 11:25-26; Eph 4:32*

___15. **Generosity**. *Deut 16:12; Ps 37:21, 41:1; Pro 3:9, 11:24, 19:17; Mt 10:42; Lk 6:38; Acts 20:35; II Cor 9:7, 13; Eph 4:28; I Tim 6:17-19* (Selfishness and greed contribute to forms of illness. Generosity increases overall well-being and especially marital happiness.)

___16. **Gifts** utilized. *Rom 12:6-8; I Cor 12.* (Spiritual and natural gifts identified and utilized.)

___17. **Goals**. *Mt 6:33; I Cor 2:2; Phil 3:13-14* Without goals we become as a wandering generality, shooting in the dark. Goals reflect desire, focus, and passion.

___18. **Growth**. *Phil 1:9; Col 1:10; I Thess 3:12; II Pt 1:5-8* Failure to grow leads to stagnation. The spirit and soul knows no limit to inner growth.

___19. **Heart Purity** out of which comes motivational purity, attitudes of Christ, perfect love. *Ps 24:3-4, 51:10; Mt 5:8; Acts 15:9; I Tim 1:5; I Pt 1:22* (800 plus references to the spiritual and moral heart.)

___20. **Hope**. *Rom 5:1-5, 15:4; Titus 2:11-13* – a by-product of faith.

___21. **Humility**. *Pro 22:4; Mic 6:8; Mt 5:5; I Pt 5:5-7; Jms 4:6*

___22. **Hunger and Thirst** for Righteousness. *Mt 5:6, 6:33* This is a spiritual priority.

___23. **Investment** and Stewardship over what we possess. *Mt 25:14-30; Lk 15:11-24; Gal 6:7* Time – Talents – Treasures. Seek to invest in a cause and purpose greater than self.

___24. **Joy** in the Lord. *Ps 5:11; Neh 8:10; Hab 3:17-18; Mt 5:10-12; Jn 15:11; Rom 12:12; I Cor 6:10; Phil 4:4; I Thess 5:16.* Constant work is required for the maintenance of Christian joy.

___25. **Justice** in Relationships. *Mic 6:8; Heb 12:14*

___26. **Kindness** in Relationships. *Eph 4:32*

___27. **Laughter/Smiling** in Relationships. *Pro 17:22.* How many times do you laugh and smile per day? We were designed to laugh and share our smile with others.

___28. **Love** in our relationship with God and people. *Mt 5:43-44, 22:37-40; Jn 13:35, 15:12; Rom 12:9-10; I Cor 13; Eph 5:1-2*

___29. **Loyalty** in relationships. *Pr 17:17*

___30. **Mercy** in Relationships. *Mt 5:7*

___31. **Moderation** – Living a self-controlled life over life's natural desires. *Ecc 2; Gal 5:22-23; Eph 5:18; Phil 4:5; II Pt 1:5-7*

____32. **Nobility** of character. Honesty and Authenticity – *Eph 4:25; I Pt 2:1-2.* Clear Conscience – *I Tim 1:5.* Moral Purity – *I Cor 6:18-20; Eph 5:3-5*

____33. **Non-Conformity** with the "world." *Rom 12:2; Jms 4:4; I Jn 2:15-17*

____34. **Non-Judgementalness.** *Mt 7:1-5*

____35. **Obedience** to God's Laws, Principles, and the Voice of the Lord. *Deut 11:26-28; Jn 14:15; Phil 4:9; I Jn 3:21-22*

____36. **Patience.** *Rom 12:12; Gal 5:22-23; II Pt 1:5-7; Phil 4:5*

____37. **Peace and Peace Making.** *Mt 5:9; Rom 12:18; Heb 12:14*

____38. **Poise**, stability and fairness in the midst of adversity. *Phil 4:5*

____39. **Purpose** for which to live. *Jer 29:11; Eph 2:10; Phil 1:21, 3:10*

____40. **Prayer.** (fasting) *I Sam 12:23; Ps 5:3; Jer 33:3; Mt 6:6, 7:7, 13; Rom 12:12; Eph 6:18; Phil 4:6; Jms 5:16*

____41. **Quietness and Rest** in the Lord. *Ps 23, 46:10; Mt 11:28; Phil 4:11*

____42. **Relational Harmony and Fellowship** within the Body of Christ. *Acts 2:46-47; Rom 12:9-10,18; Phil 2:1-4; Heb 12:14* We are to practice the many "one another" statements in the New Testament.

____43. **Responsibility** for our choices, activities, thoughts, speech. *Rom 14:12; Gal 6:7*

____44. **Sensitivity** to people and their feelings and needs. *Rom 12:15; Eph 4:32*

____45. **Sensitivity** to the moving and ministry of the Holy Spirit. *Eph 4:30; I Thess 5:19*

____46. **Spirit-Filled Life** which exudes the Fruit of the Spirit and the Power of God. *Acts 1:8; Gal 5:22-23, Eph 1:19, 3:20, 5:18-22. (*Not fleshly driven.)

____47. **Singing** and "*making melody in your heart to the Lord." Acts 16:25; Eph 5:18-19; Ps 40:1-3, 98:1, 4-8.*

____48. **Submission** to God's Voice, Will, Way, Word, Authority. *Jms 4:7*

____49. **Tamed Tongue.** Speak words of blessing, faith, affirmation, inspiration, thanksgiving, hope, optimism, praise, expectancy, love, joy and peace. *Ps 19:14, 34:1, 141:3; Pro 10:11, 12:18, 15:4, 18:21; Mt 12:34, 36-37; Eph 4:29; Col 4:6, Jms 3:3-10.* Words contain tremendous creative, connective, and magnetic powers. We live in the realm and power of our words. Words convey our thoughts and reflect our attitude. How many words do you speak per day, and are they more positive than negative, more of a blessing or a curse (attack, demeaning, destructive, etc.)?

____50. **Thankfulness.** *Ps 100:4; Phil 4:6; I Thess 5:18*

___51. **Unity** of spirit within self, the Body of Christ, others, and God.

___52. **Victory** by faith over the world. *Deut 20:4; Josh 1:9; Isa 54:17; Jn 16:33; Rom 8:31; I Cor 15:27; II Cor 2:14; Eph 6:10, 13; Phil 4:13; I Jn 5:4*

___53. **Will of God pursued and obeyed.** *Mt 6:10, 7:21-23; Rom 12:2; Eph 5:17; I Thess 4:3*

___54. **Wisdom** of God pursued. *I Kgs 3:9; Ps 119:97-98; Pro 4:5-7, 9:10; Jms 1:5-6*

___55. **Word of God.** Ingested and Digested. Read it, Study it, Meditate Upon it. *Josh 1:7; Ps 1:1-3, 119:11, 105; Pro 4:20-23; II Tim 3:16-17*

___56. **Worship of God.** *Ex 23:25; Ps 29:2, 95:6, 99:5, 100:4; Jn 4:24* Worship brings: **Rest** to our Bodies, **Refreshment** to our soul and spirit, and **Renewal** to our mind.

___57. **Work.** *Gen 2:15; Ex 20:9; Pro 12:11, 24, 13:4, 14:23; I Tim 5:8.*
We are designed to work, if able, and to do that which helps ourselves, others, and the work of the Lord.

___58. **X-Out** the negative past of which we have no control and seek to live for the now and the future. *Phil 3:13-14* Don't dwell on past failures, enemies, defeats, crises, broken dreams, adversities, or losses. Believe your todays and tomorrows will be better than your yesterdays.

___59. **Yielded-ness** of body, soul, and spirit to the Lordship of Christ. *Rom 12:1; I Thess 5:23*
This is total consecration.

___60. **Zeal** and enthusiasm for the Lord and life. *Rom 12:11*
How much zeal (fire) and enthusiasm do you have for the Lord and His work?

Add up your subjective score_____

You are encouraged to list the "virtues" you believe to be in need of personal enrichment, following the completion of the above evaluation. You may also wish to have your spouse or a close associate assist you with this spiritual evaluation. *Ps 139:23-24*

Chapter 4

The Blessings of God and Major Keys to His Blessings

The concept of blessing is in some form or fashion referenced nearly 700 times throughout the Bible, with 410 specific references "to bless" or "to be blessed."

A. Four Categories of Blessings
The Biblical subject of blessing can be divided into 4 major categories.

1. God Blessing People
It is a fascinating study to observe how God bestowed special blessings upon certain people throughout the Bible. You are challenged to observe God's blessings bestowed upon the following Bible characters.
> Job *1, 2*
> Abraham – *Gen 12:1-3, 15:5, 17:5-6, 24:1*
> Isaac – *Gen 26:3, 12, 24*
> Jacob – *Gen 27:27-29, 28:12-15*
> Moses – *Ex 3, 4*
> *Joshua* – Josh 1:9; (Bk of Joshua)
> Samson – *Judg 14:19*
> Gideon – *Judg 6, 7*
> David – *I Sam 16*
> Solomon – *I Kgs 2:45, 3*
> Mary – *Lk 1:26-38*
> People who tithe – *Mal 3:8-12*

2. *People Blessing God – Ps 34:1, 103:1-5*

3. *People Blessing People – Num 6:25-26*
> Isaac blessing Jacob – *Gen 27:28-29; Heb 11:20*
> Jacob blessing his sons – *Gen 49; Heb 11:20*
> Moses blessing the 12 tribes of Israel – *Deut 33*
> Jesus blessing children – *Mk 10:13-16*
> People blessing enemies – *Mt 5:43-44; Rom 12:14*

4. God and People Blessing Things
> God blessing His creation – *Gen 1:20-22*
> Solomon praying a blessing from God upon the Temple – *I Kgs 8:22-30*
> Jesus blessing the fish and bread to feed 5000 men plus women and
> children – *Mk 6:41*
> (We have the right to pray a blessing upon a church building, home, car,
> field, etc.)

While there are four categories of blessings presented in scripture, the focus of this study is centered around God's desire and provision to bless His people. This is especially presented in *Deut 28:1-14*, in which God clearly states that He will bless His people if they will keep His commandments. This promise applies to anyone who elects to serve God with their whole heart and life, and obey His commandments and principles.

There are two major Hebrew words in the Old Testament, *barak* and *esher,* which convey the idea of "blessing or to bless," along with the thought of happiness.

The two major New Testament Greek words *makarios* (happiness), and *eulogeo* convey the concept of blessing in the context of good will, happiness, or good report.

Closely aligned with the theme of God's blessing is the concept of God's favor, and His smile upon the "bless-ables."

These three attitudes and actions of God toward the righteous are observed in the following scriptures.

a) God's Blessings:
    II Chr 16:9; Deut 11:26-28, 30:19; Josh 1:8; Job 22:21; Ps 1:1-3, 5:11, 16:11, 28:1, 4-5, 34:7, 35:27, 37:4-23, 84:11, 92:12, 14, 115:13-14; Pro 3:1-10, 22:4; Isa 54:17, 58:11; Jer 29:11, 33:3; Mt 5:3-12, 6:33; Jn 10:10, 15:2; Phil 4:19; III Jn 2.

    There are many examples of God's special blessings upon His people throughout both the Old and New Testaments, as already stated. But we need to ask ourselves: "Am I one of God's blessable servants?"

b) God's Favor: Closely aligned with God's blessings is God's favor. Receiving God's favor means God's approval, acceptance, grace, and mercy has been extended to a spiritually designated person.

    Review the following list of Bible characters who were singled out to receive God's special favor.

    Gen 6:8 "Noah found favor in the eyes of the Lord"
    Ex 33:17 God to Moses *"…you have found favor in my sight, and I know you by name."*
    Lk 1:28 An angel to Mary *"…Hail thou that art highly favored. The Lord is with thee. Blessed art thou among women."*
    Lk 2:52 "And Jesus increased in wisdom and stature, and in favor with God and man."
    Acts 7:45-46 "…David; who found favor before God…"
    Ps 5:12 "For thou Lord will bless the righteous; with favor wilt thou compass him as with a shield."
    Ps 90:17 "May the favor of the Lord our God rest on us…"
    Pro 3:4 "So shalt thou find favor and good understanding in the sight of God and man."
    Pro 3:34 "…to the humble he giveth favor."
    Pro 8:35 "For he who finds me finds life and obtains favor from the Lord."
    Pro 12:2 "A good man will obtain favor from the Lord."

c) *God's Smile:* Someone has said, "If we have the smile of God, we can survive the frowns of people." God's smile reflects His pleasure derived from His servants.

    Num 6:25 "…The Lord make his face shine (smile) on you."
    Ps 67:1 "God be gracious to us, and bless us and make his face to shine upon us."
    Ps 80:3 "Turn us again, O God, and cause thy face to shine; and we shall be saved."
    Ps 119:35 "Make thy face to shine (smile) upon thy servant."

Combined Definition: The definition of these three responses of God toward the righteous can be summarized as follows:

> Accept, approve, anoint,
> Bestow favor upon,
> Cherish, cultivate to the fullest,
> Delight in, defend, protect,
> Elevate, enrich, encourage, extend extra kindness and good will,
> Find pleasure in, to cause to flourish,
> Give grace unto, give special regard to, to give preferential treatment,
> Help, honor, to make happy,
> Increase in influence, contribution, effectiveness, quality and quantity of life,
> To promote.

B. God's Blessings and the Sources from Which They Come

God's special blessings come through various sources and channels of life. The following list appears to reflect the major ways God manifests His blessings upon His people.

1. Providential Acts of God working for us—not against us.
   God's providence refers to God's care, protection, guidance, and intervention on our behalf. It is the unfolding of God's will in our life. *Acts 9; Rom 8:28*
2. Plan of Redemption—and all the benefits that pertain to it. *Eph 1:7*
3. Purpose for which we were designed. *Jer 29:11; Eph 2:10; Phil 2:13*
4. Prayers offered and answered. *Jms 5:16; Jer 33:3*
5. Peace of God within. *Phil 4:6-7*
6. Principles and laws of God, if obeyed, will bring positive results in life. *Deut 11:26-28*
7. Power of God at work within us. Power of Faith, the Word, Holy Spirit, Resurrection, Prayers, etc. *Lk 24:49; Acts 1:8, 4:31-32; Eph 3:20, 6:10; II Tim 1:7*
8. Provisions of God extended to us in time of need. *Mt 6:33; Phil 4:19*
9. Promises of God claimed by faith *II Pt 1:4; Rom 15:4*
10. Protection of God around and over us. *Ps 34:7; Isa 54:17*
11. Personal gifts bestowed upon us. *Rom 12:5-8; I Cor 12*
12. People brought into our life, such as our spouse, family, friends, strangers, etc.

C. The Major Keys to God's Blessings

There are many factors that contribute to the blessings, the favor, and the smile of God upon His people. A careful study of this subject indicates that there are certain key virtues that serve as the fundamental foundation for God's special blessings.

1. Fear of God – *Pro 1:7, 9:10, 14:27, 19:23, 22:4; Ps 128:1, 4,, 33:18, 115:13-14, 147:11*

   There are at least 147 references to the "fear of the Lord or God" in the Bible. One of the key verses is *Psa 147:11* which reads, *"The Lord takes pleasure in them that fear Him."* Another important verse to remember is *Ecc 12:13*, which declares the whole duty of man is to, "Fear God and keep his commandments." (*Ecc 5:7*)
   To fear the Lord represents a holy attitude, view, and response toward God. It can mean any one or more of the following:

   > Faith in God
   > Focus on God
   > Exaltation of God

Acknowledgement of God with awe and wonder
Awareness that God is aware of our total words, actions, intentions,
      thoughts, emotions, desires
Respect and reverence for God's:

Judgments	Way
Authority	Will
Power	Word
Name	Wrath
Nature	

      Submission to God
      Honor of God
      Praise, Thanksgiving and Worship of God

We reflect the "fear of God" through our:
      Treatment of His Name – *Ex 20:7; Lev 18:21; Ps 8:1; Mt 6:9*
      Reverence and Respect for the holy and sacred – *Lev 19:2, 30, 26:2;*
         Ez 22:26; Heb 12:28-29
      Acknowledgement of God in all our ways – *Pro 3:6*
      Choices we make – *Josh 24:15*
      Conception of Sin – *Rom 12:9; I Thess 5:23* Sin is to be hated and
         avoided.
      Treatment of others – *Rom 12:10, 13-18; Eph 4:32; Phil 2:3*
      Obedience to God's laws – *Deut 11:26-28; Jn 14:13; I Jn 3:21-22*
      Respect for life – *Ex 20:13; Lk 18:20; Mt 18:5-6*
      Speech – *Ps 19:14, 34:1; Pro 18:21; Eph 4:29*
      Priorities – *Mt 6:33*
      Attitude toward life – *Ps 34:1, 103:1-5; Phil 2:14-15; I Thess 5:18*
      Thoughts – *Josh 1:8; Ps 1:1-3, 19:14, 139:23-24; Isa 26:3;*
         II Cor 10:5
      Submission to authority (both God & man) – *Mt 6:9-10; Eph 5:21;*
         I Pt 5:5-7

The Bible frequently refers to the spiritual benefits derived from the "fear of the Lord." Listed below are a few of these benefits found in Psalms and Proverbs.

Psalms
34:7 It brings angelic protection and God's deliverance.
103:11 It brings God's mercy.
103:13 It brings God's pity.
145:19 It brings fulfillment of God given desires.
147:11 It brings pleasure to God.

Proverbs
1:7 "It is the beginning of knowledge."
9:10 "It is the beginning of wisdom."
3:5-8 It benefits the body.
10:27 It extends life.
14:26 It brings confidence and a refuge.
24:27 It is a fountain of life.
19:23 It brings satisfaction.

Remember, Job was a man blessed mightily by God, and Satan acknowledged this spiritual reality in Job's life. Please take note that *Job 1:1* gives a concise description of his moral characteristics by stating that he was a man who was *"morally blameless, upright, feared God, and hated evil."*

God still honors anyone who is upright in character and has the fear of God within the heart. The blessing of God may not be in material wealth, but be assured there will be a special blessing, in some form or fashion, bestowed upon the righteous. *Ps 5:12, 92:12, 14*

Whoever has the "fear of God" within their heart is well on their way to receiving God's special blessings. This is a basic step toward a "bless-able" life.

Any person, society, or nation that excludes this spiritual disposition from their moral base will invite spiritual demise upon their life and land.

Any person or nation who excludes the "fear of God" will be inclined toward greater:
> Disregard for life
> Rebellion against authority
> Immorality
> Violence and murder
> Evil manifestations
> Hopelessness and futility

The Apostle Paul speaks to this reality in his summary of man's sinful nature and moral degeneration, when he wrote, *"There is no fear of God before their eyes."* *Rom 3:18*

2. Faith in God and His Promises
   Key Scriptures: *Hab 2:4; Pr 3:5-6; Ps 37:3-5; Mt 8:13, 9:22, 29, 17:20, 19:26; Lk 1:37; Mk 9:23; Jn 20:29; Acts 6:5, 11:24; Rom 1:16-17, 4:20-21, 5:1,10:17, 12:3 Gal 3:11; Heb 10:38, 11:1, 6; I Jn 5:4*

   The law of faith supersedes all laws within the universe. This law is governed by principles that exceed the principles that govern the physical world. This is how miracles take place.
   Some concept of faith or lack thereof appears over 500 times in the New Testament, with the use of 5 different Greek words. Faith is that spiritual entity within the heart that serves as:
   > That which pleases God *Heb 11:5-6*
   > The Bridge between the physical and spiritual worlds
   > The Connector between us and God
   > The Channel through which God works in and through our life
   > The Spiritual Circumference zone around us in which God works within and through our life
   > The Spiritual ability to perceive, believe, imagine, think, and to sense in our spirit that God is at work, both in the spiritual and physical world within us and around us and in the lives of others
   > The Spiritual ability to discern to some degree within our spirit that which is going on within the spiritual world around us and within us
   > *Elisha – II Kgs 6:17*

The Spiritual ability to see within our spirit that which is not as though it is *Rom 4:17*

The greater our faith, the greater the pleasure of God upon us. Therefore, it should be the desire of every born again believer to build up their faith in God. Here are some ways to increase faith:

Factor the Word of God into your thinking. Remember the words of the Apostle Paul, *"...faith cometh by hearing, and hearing by the Word of God." Rom 10:17* Seek to memorize key promises of God's Word which serve as a stimulus to faith. *Rom 15:4, 8:28, 31*

Ask continuously in prayer for God's help, enlightenment, leadership, and power for each day's challenges and needs. *Jer 33:3; Mt 6:6, 7:7; I Thess 5:17; Phil 4:6-7; Jms 5:16*

Alignment with people of great faith e.g. *Acts 6:8 (Stephen); Acts 11:24 (Barnabas)*

Incorporate patience as you wait on the Lord's answers and intervention. *Ps 37:7; Isa 40:31*

Incorporate into your thinking the complexity and vastness of the Universe *(Ps 8, 19, 139)* Reflect on the reality that astronomers estimate there are at least 2 trillion galaxies in the Universe with between 300 or 400 billion stars in each and God knows them all by name. *Ps 147:4; Isa 40:26*

Trust in the Lord's: (Don't worry)
        Providence – *Rom 8:28*
        Plan of Redemption – *Col 1:9-14; Eph 1:3-23*
        Purposes for your life – *Jer 29:11*
        Prayer Response – *Jer 33:3; Phil 4:6*
        Peace – *Phil 4:7; Jn 14:27*
        Power – *Eph 3:20; Phil 4:13*
        Provisions – *Phil 4:19*
        Promises – *II Pt 1:4; Rom 15:4*
        Protection – *Isa 54:17*

Hope in God and live in the spirit of:
        Hope (which comes out of faith)
        Optimism
        Praise
        Expectancy

3. Humility before God and others – *Pr 22:4; Mic 6:8; II Chron 7:14; Mt 5:5, 18:1-4; Phil 2:5-8; Jms 4:6; I Pt 5:5-6*

Humility is a prerequisite to entering into the Kingdom of God. It is the ability to reject personal pride and come under the authority of an Almighty God.

Pride is characterized by:
Arrogance
Belittling others
Promotion of self
Rebellion and defiance against authority
Independence from God
Envy of others
Any attempt to place self above God's Will, Way and Word
Any attempt to exclude God from one's self
Any attempt to diminish God so as to promote self

Humility is the ability to:
Be teachable and thankful
Elevate and esteem others more than self and have an appropriate
    evaluation of self – *Rom 12:3*
Be accountable
Be correctable
Be honest
Be apologetic
Be benevolent
Be loving
Be empathetic
Be submissive – *Job 22:21 NIV*
Be servant-like
Be self-denying
Be patient

James reflects the significance of a humble spirit when he wrote *"God resisteth the proud, but giveth grace unto the humble." Jms 4:6*

It is God's specialty to:
Take the nobodies of life and make them into somebodies
Take the weak and make them strong
Take the lowly and exalt them to a higher level of life.

One of the greatest verses that conveys the importance of humility is found in *Pro 22:4* which reads, *"By humility and the fear of the Lord, are riches, and honor, and life."*

4. Alive in Christ brought about by a Personal Spiritual Resurrection – *Jn 3:1-7; II Cor 5:17; Eph 2:1, 4:22-24; Col 1:13-14, 3:1-4; Phil 1:21*
We are spiritually dead by nature, but through Christ's physical death and resurrection, provision was made for our spiritual resurrection.

Spiritual life is imparted when we, by faith, confess Christ as Lord, confess and repent of our sins, and submit ourselves to the authority of an Almighty God. This spiritual resurrection brings about a new nature, for we have been born again by the Spirit of God. *Jn 3:1-7*

This spiritual experience brings a spiritual benefit package which includes:
>Forgiveness of sins
>Regeneration and redemption of the heart
>Adoption into the family of God
>Cleansing from all sin
>Kingdom of heaven within
>Spirit's witness that we are a child of God, along with additional blessings beyond measure

5. Infilling of the Spirit and Heart Purity (Commitment and consecration to Christ) – *II Chron 16:9; Ps 24:3-4, 51:10, 139:23-24; Mt 5:8; Lk 24:49; Acts 1:5, 8, 2:4, 4:31, 15:9, 19:1-6; Rom 12:2; Phil 1:21, 3:10-11; I Tim 1:5; I Pt 1:22; I Jn 3:2-3*

The Bible refers to the spiritual heart over 800 times. Heart purity is experienced when the believer totally surrenders to the Lordship of Christ by an act of complete consecration subsequent to the new birth experience. *Jn 3:1-7; Rom 12:1-2; Phil 3:10-11.* This relinquishment of self to God's complete control allows for the Spirit's infilling, and cleansing from the principle of sin that resides within the "heart" of man from birth until the moment of compete sanctification of spirit, soul, and body. *(I Thess 5:23)* This principle of sin contains basic sinful forces that make man's nature vulnerable to sinful temptations and the rejection of God and His moral laws.

The acts of sin are forgiven when we seek, by faith, God's forgiveness and accept Christ as our Savior. But the root of sin still exists within the heart. Paul (and the Hebrew writer) referred to this sin principle by using various metaphors and figures of speech, such as:
>*"The Besetting Sin" – Heb 12:l*
>*"The Body of Death" – Rom 7:24*
>*"The Body of Sin" – Rom 6:6*
>*"The Carnal Mind" – Rom 8:7*
>*"Enmity within" – Rom 7:21*
>*"The Flesh (Sarx)" – Gal 5:17*
>*"The Law of Sin which is in my members" – Rom 7:23*
>*"Our Old Man (self)" – Rom 6:6; Eph 4:22; Col 3:9*
>*"Root of Bitterness" – Heb 12:15*
>*"The Sin" – Rom 6:12*
>*"Sin that dwelleth in me" –Rom 7:17,20*
>*"The sin in the flesh" – Rom 8:3*
>*"Uncleanness" – Rom 6:19*

Again, this sinful principle contains multiple sinful forces within the heart, which serve as motivators to sin and violate the laws of God.

(See Addendum I – Basic Sinful Forces Within the Sinful and Carnal Heart).

There is a tremendous emphasis within the scriptures about possessing a "heart" that is cleansed from this inner root of sin.

Review carefully the following verses that pertain to the purity and moral wholesomeness of the "heart." *II Chron 16:9; Ps 24:3-4, 51:10; Mt 5:8; Acts 15:9; I Tim 1:5; II Tim 2:22; I Pt 1:22; Phil 1:10 (pure and blameless); I Jn 3:2-3*

A careful study of the Hebrew and Greek words used within the above scriptures convey the strong message that the "heart" is to possess the moral quality of:

> Purity
> Unmixed motives
> No duplicity
> Transparency and blamelessness
> Wholeness - completeness

> When the biblical writers addressed the action required to remove this sinful force from the heart, they always used strong and decisive words such as:
> > To abolish – *Eph 2:15; Is 2:18*
> > To cleanse – *I Jn 1:7*
> > To circumcise – *Col 2:11*
> > To crucify – *Rom 6:6*
> > To destroy – *I Jn 3:8*
> > To free from sin- *Rom 6:22*
> > To kill or put to death
> > To mortify – *Col 3:5; Rom 8:13*
> > To purge – *II Tim 2:21*
> > To put off – *Eph 4:22; Col 3:8*
> > To root up – *Col 2:11; Mt 15:13*
> > To sanctify – *Jn 17:17; I Thess 5:23; Heb 13:12*
> > To take away – *I Jn 3:4-10*

These words do not indicate that the removal of this "root of sin" occurs through progressive action, but rather through a decisive and crisis action within.

We will never function at our best, or fully realize all the blessings God has in store for the pure in heart, until this spiritual issue is resolved.

Every born again believer is to seek God for an inner cleansing that removes the "principle of sin" from the "heart." This can only be attained through a sincere "hunger and thirst" after God's righteousness, and a total surrender of our will to God's will. It involves a complete commitment and consecration to the Lordship of Christ, including all of our:

> Affections
> Ambitions
> Aspirations
> Associations

Heart purity represents the removal of all carnal disposition from the "heart," thus allowing for inner harmony with God, self, and others, and the total infilling of the Spirit. *Eph 5:18* This experience is called "holiness of heart," from which flows:

> Motivational purity – *Mt 5:48*
> Attitudes of Christ – *Phil 2:4-8*
> Perfect love – *I Jn 4:17; Jn 13:35, 15:12; I Cor 13*

It is this kind of inner purity and power that enables the "saved and sanctified" believer to live a holy and spiritually powerful lifestyle in a sinful and problematic world.

6. Biblical Thinking Filled with Biblical Promises – *Josh 1:8; Ps 1:1-3, 119:97; Pro 4:20-23, 23:7; Isa 26:3; Jn 15:7; II Cor 10:5; Phil 4:8; Col 3:2, 16; Rom 15:4; II Pt 1:4*

Our secular society teaches us to think secular and worldly thoughts. The Bible teaches us to think Biblical thoughts within our mind that has been renewed and quickened by the Spirit of God and His Word.

The Book of Proverbs conveys the importance of incorporating God's Word into our thinking. *Pro 4:20-23, 23:7.*

God promised Joshua great success if he would ingest and meditate on God's Word Josh 1:8.

The Psalmist repeated this promise when he wrote, *"Blessed is the man…(whose) delight is in the law of the Lord; and in his law doth he meditate (chew it over and over) day and night…and whatsoever he doeth shall prosper." Ps 1:1-3*

The Bible repeatedly states that the more our thought life is centered around God's Word, the greater will be the blessings of God upon our life.

7. Obedience to the Laws, Commandments, and Principles of God's Word
    When God established the nation of Israel, He gave a powerful promise. He empathetically stated that if His people would obey and keep His commandments, they would be blessed as a nation, and as a people. Their enemies would never be victorious over them. *Deut 11:26-28, 28:1-14, 15-20, 30:19.*

This theme of obedience and divine blessing is paramount throughout the scriptures. Jesus referred to it when He told the disciples, *"If you love me, keep my commandments."* Their obedience would bring the blessing of His prayer for the Father to give them the Holy Spirit. *Jn 14:15-16.*

Jesus also spoke to His critics about the importance of hearing and keeping the Word of God, when He said, *"…blessed are they that hear the Word of God and keep it." Lk 11:28*

John references this thought in *I Jn 3:22* when he wrote, *"And whatsoever we ask, we receive of him, because we keep his commandments and do those things that are pleasing in his sight."*

Obedience is an absolute essential for anyone who desires the blessing, favor, and smile of God upon their life.

8. Acknowledgement of God in all our Ways – *Ps 16:11; Pro 3:6; I Cor 10:31; Col 3:17*
    The word *"acknowledge"* in *Pro 3:6* comes from the Hebrew word *"yada,"* which conveys the idea of coming to know someone by observing, reflecting, and experiencing that person. We, therefore, can conclude that the closer we are to God and His Word, the more inclined we are to observe God in our life and in the world around us.

The greater our Christian faith and maturity in Christ, the greater our spiritual ability to acknowledge and recognize that God is at work in all of life. Especially in the life of every "faith driven Christian" whose heart and mind has been illuminated by the Spirit of God.

The promise that follows this spiritual mandate to *"acknowledge God in all our ways,"* is that God will *"direct our paths."* Here is a clear reference to God's providential actions within our life. We are given the assurance that if our faith is strong enough to "acknowledge" that God is at work in our life, and in the life of others, He will lead us into truth, opportunities, and relationships in keeping with His will.

This Divine leadership assures us of His blessings, favor, and smile of approval upon us.

There are numerous ways by which we can acknowledge God throughout every day of our life. We can acknowledge Him when we:

> Awaken in the morning and declare, *"This is the day the Lord hath made, we will rejoice and be glad in it." Ps 118:24*

> Recognize that *"Every good gift and every perfect (free) gift is from above, and cometh down from the Father of lights…" Jms 1:17*

> Thankfully express gratitude for each new day, gifts of life, food, etc. *I Thess 5:18*

> Seek His Will, Way and Word through prayer.

> Seek God's blessing and protection upon our life, marriage, family, friends, and church.
> Recognize that He is a God of:
>> Providential action
>> Plan of redemption and its benefits
>> Purpose for which to live
>> Prayer Response to our prayers – *Jer 33:3; Phil 4:6-7*
>> Peace – *Jn 14:27*
>> Principles and Laws – *Deut 11:26-28*
>> Power – *Acts 1:8; Phil 4:13*
>> Provision for personal needs – *Phil 4:19*
>> Promises – *II Pt 1:4*
>> Protection – *Isa 54:17*
>> Preparation for our eternal future – *Jn 14:1-3*
>> Provision of personal gifts – *Rom 12:3, 6-8*
>> Provision of people needed to fulfill God's will in our life.

Always remember, the more we acknowledge God in all of our ways, the greater our faith, and God's blessings upon our life.

9. Delight in the Lord – Ps 37:4 – to find pleasure in knowing, obeying, and serving
   God.

10. Generosity – *Deut 14:22-28, 15:10; Ps 41:1-3; Pro 3:9-10, 11:24, 19:17; Mal 3:10; Lk 6:38; II Cor 9:7; Eph 4:28*
Generosity is a characteristic of God's nature, for He is a God of benevolence. It is also a trait of the righteous, for it is stated in *Ps 37:21 "...the righteous showeth mercy and giveth."*

The Bible is filled with references to our giving to God and to those in need. A close study of many of these scriptures reveals that giving brings special blessings upon the giver. For example, Jesus said, *"Give and it shall be given unto you; good measure, pressed down, and shaken together, and running over..." Lk 6:38*

Pro 11:24 states, "The world of the generous gets larger and larger; the world of the stingy gets smaller and smaller." MSG

There are numerous spiritual and secular studies regarding the benefits derived from giving. The following findings are the common results seen throughout scientific studies of those who practice a charitable lifestyle.
> Increased overall happiness
> Increased health—physically and mentally
> Increased relational harmony
> Increased self-worth
> Increased purpose for which to live
> Increased longevity
> Decreased depression

Paul told the Corinthian Church that *"...God loves a cheerful giver" II Cor 9:7;* not the reluctant of heart. No greedy or covetous person can expect God's special blessings or favor upon their life.

11. Prayer – I Sam 12:23; *Jer 33:3; Ps 5:3; Pro 15:29; Mt 6:6, 7:7, 11; Eph 6:18; Phil 4:6; Col 4:2; I Thess 5:17; I Tim 2:8; Jms 5:16*

The Bible contains 375 specific references to prayer and 377 references to praise and 222 recorded prayers. There are at least 25 references in the Gospels about Jesus' prayer life. He taught His disciples the value and importance of prayer, both by His words and example.

The need to pray appears to be a universal instinct within the heart. The evidence of praying is indicated in every culture and society. Studies reveal that the American Christian averages 3 to 7 minutes in prayer per day, including prayers of thanks for food. PEW Research shares the following percentages about prayer:
> 64% of Christians pray more than once per day
> 63% of Christians pray on a regular basis
> 64% of women pray every day
> 45% of men pray every day

The benefits of prayer have been studied spiritually and scientifically. The conclusions are impressive.

Spiritual Benefits of Prayer
Connects us with God through faith – *Ps 32:1-5*
Protects us from the evil forces of the devil, world, the flesh, and temptation
Mt 26:41; Eph 6:10-18
Reinforces our faith – *Mt 17:20-21*
Releases us from cares, anxieties, and worries – *Phil 4:6; I Pt 5:7*
Energizes and empowers our spirit and spiritual life – *Lk 18:1; Acts 4:31; Eph 3:20*
Activates and invokes God's special blessings, favor, and power upon us, others, and God's work – *Jer 33:3; I Chron 4:10; Acts 12:5*
Aligns us with God's Spirit, will, way, and Word – *Rom 8:26-27*
Moves us closer to God, and God closer to us – *Jms 4:8*
Negates the power of sin and Satan – *Jms 4:7; Eph 4:27, 6:18*
Supports overall health-- physically, mentally, emotionally, socially, spiritually

Physical and Psychological Benefits of Prayer
Prayer Increases:
Serenity of heart
Happiness
Harmony and forgiveness in relationships
Relaxation
Immunity
Inner strength
Likeability
Longevity
Energy level

Prayer Decreases:
Hospital stays
Stress
Surgical recovery time, especially heart surgery
Aging issues
Blood pressure
Emotional issues (grief, anger, envy, etc.)

It is of special interest that the spiritual life of effective prayer warriors will always include the first 10 major keys to God's blessings:
Fear of God
Faith
Humility
Alive in Christ
Infilling of the Spirit and Purity of Heart
Biblical Thinking
Obedience
Acknowledgement of God in all their ways
Delight in the Lord
Generosity

The following outline of "prayer essentials and guidelines" is provided for a quick review of the basic keys to an effective prayer life.

PRAYER ESSENTIALS AND GUIDELINES

FEAR OF THE LORD (147 references) – Pro 1:7, 9:10, 22:4; Ps 145:19, 115:13-14

✝

FAITH IN GOD AND HIS WORD – Heb 11:6; Mt 8:13, 9:22, 29; Acts 6:5,8; 11:24

✝

HUMILITY OF SPIRIT – II Chron 7:14; I Pt 5:5-7; Pr 22:4

✝

ALIVE IN CHRIST – Jn 3:1-7; Col 3:1-4; II Cor 5:17

✝

FILLED WITH THE SPIRIT – Eph 5:18

✝

BIBLICAL THINKING (Promises) – Josh 1:8; Ps 1:1-3; Rom 10:17, 15:4; II Pt 1:4

(God's Providence – Plan of Redemption – Purpose – Prayer Response –
Peace – Principles – Power – Provision – Promises – Protection – Prophecies –
Preparation for Eternal Dwelling)

✝

OBEDIENCE TO GOD'S LAWS/PRINCIPLES – Deut 11:26-28; Jn 14:15; I Jn 3:21-22

✝

ACKNOWLEDGEMENT OF GOD IN ALL YOUR WAYS – Pro 3:5-6

✝

DELIGHT YOURSELF IN THE LORD – "and He shall give you the desires (petitions) of your heart" - Ps 37:4

✝

INTEGRITY OF HEART (Heart Purity) – Ps 24:3-5, 66:18; Mt 5:8; II Tim 2:22; I Pt 1:22, 3:16;
James 5:16; I Jn 3:21-22

✝

INTENSITY OF DESIRE – Ps 37:3-5, 145:19; Mk 11:24; I Jn 5:13-14
(Dream it and Visualize it)

+

INTENSITY OF PRAYER – Jer 29:13; Mt 7:7, 17:20-21

+

HONORING KEY PRAYER PRINCIPLES

Praying in the Spirit – Rom 8:26-27	Praying Specifically – Mt 17:20-21
Praying in the Name of Jesus – Jn 14:13-14	Praying Unselfishly – James 4:3
Praying in the Will of God – I Jn 5:13-14	Praying Persistently – Mt 7:7; Lk 11:5-10
Praying in the Spirit of, Forgiveness & Reconciliation – Mt 5:23-24	Praying in Partnership – Mt 18:19-20
Praying in Keeping with God's Love, Laws & Principles	Praying with Fasting – Mt 17:20-21

+

FAITH PUT INTO WORDS – Mt 17:20; Mk 11:23-24 = Prayer Results

Conclusion:

The many prayer references in the Bible gives evidence that prayer is essential to our overall spiritual and psychological well-being, and the receiving of God's special blessings.

Also, past and present scientific studies reveal conclusively that prayer brings significant overall health benefits.

In light of the above truth, the question needs to be asked, "Why is it that so little time is given to prayer?" The following is a list of common hindrances to an effective prayer life:

Asking is an issue
    Pride
    Unworthiness
    Taught never to ask

Broken Relationships and unattended unforgiveness—*Mt 5:23-24, 6:14-15; Mk 11:25-26*
Busy-ness
Commitment Deficit
Discipline Deficit
Emotional Issues – depression – anxiety – intimacy
Faulty Faith
Focus issues: Attention Deficit Disorder (ADD); Hyperactivity or too task-oriented

Guilt
Impatience
Ingratitude
Insensitivity to the Spirit
Marital discord – *I Pt 3:7*
Non-compliance with prayer principles. When you pray, always ask, "Is my prayer
 in keeping with God's law, love, will, selflessness, and importunity?"
Selfishness (wrong motive)
Sin – *Ps 66:18*
Worldly mindedness
Worry – *Phil 4:6*

12. Forgiveness – *Mt 6:12, 14:15, 18:21-22; Mk 11:25; Lk 6:37, 15:20-24 (picture of
 forgiveness); Eph 4:32; Col 13:13*

   A. Definition: Greek word for forgiveness is *aphiemi* which means to set free. This word
      appears 17 times in the New Testament. Forgiveness also includes:
         To pardon
         To let go
         To cancel out
         To release (anger, bitterness, resentment, revenge, judgment to God)

   B. Christian forgiveness is a:
         Choice to rid self of anger, bitterness, resentment, revenge toward an
         offender

         Covenant to have a change of attitude – a resolve to let the offense go,
         never to be brought up again.

         Chance taken toward the offender

         Commitment to obey God's command to:
               Forgive
               Love with agape love
               Bless
               Pray for
               Do good unto

         Cleansing from:
               Anger
               Bitterness
               Resentment
               Revenge
               Judgment

   C. Benefits
      1. Freedom from a painful past
      2. Release from revenge and
      3. Reduction of stress

4. Ends self-defeating emotions and behaviors – (anger, bitterness, criticalness, depression, emptiness, fear)
5. Enhances health – physically, mentally, emotionally, socially, spiritually
6. Satisfies the command of God to forgive
7. Satisfies the mind with peace and serenity of mind
8. Span of life increased

D. Forgiveness is NOT:
1. Forgetting – for it will always be a part of the memory bank
2. Acquittal – for acquittal says it didn't happen
3. Always instantaneous – sometimes it requires a process with a moment of completion in mind.

E. Reasons for forgiveness struggles
1. Hurt thought to be too great
2. Anger not resolved
3. Revenge – to get even
4. Pride – I'm too good to be hurt
5. Protection from future hurt
6. Perfectionism – "It's supposed to be a perfect world."
7. Parents never really forgave – Children never experienced true forgiveness
8. Sympathy, self-pity, play out the victim's role
9. Offender must first say, "I am sorry" – conditional forgiveness

F. Evidence of forgiveness
1. Release of all ill feelings toward the offender
2. Reject talking against the offender
3. Rejoices in offender's successes
4. Regrets offender's failures or losses
5. Receptive to loving, praying for, and blessing the offender
6. Resolve to continue to choose to forgive when tempted to let go of forgiveness.

Conclusion: Unforgiveness will always block the flow of God's forgiveness, blessings, love, and mercy upon the unforgiving heart.

(Refer to Addendum II for a list of those whom God specifically blesses.)

Chapter 5

The Biblical Lifestyle and Characteristics that Complement our Essential Spiritual Virtues and Honors God's Blessings Upon Us

Throughout the New Testament there are "clusters" of Christian characteristics and virtues by which we are to live. They identify a lifestyle that not only reflects and complements the blessings of God upon our life, and the moral components by which we were designed, but also a lifestyle that brings glory to God, and quality to our spiritual character.

It is of special interest that each of these clusters of Christian ideals are always presented in the context of a problematic condition or situation.

The following New Testament clusters are worthy of serious consideration, if we desire to invoke and honor the blessings of God upon our life so that we, in turn, can reflect the life of Christ in a problematic world.

A. *Matthew 5:3-12*
      Author: Matthew, a chosen disciple of Christ
      Date: Early in Christ's ministry
      Place of Delivery: Uncertain mountain
      Problem: Sin to be confronted and resolved through the righteousness of God –
          Mt 5:6, 20, 48
      Theme: Description of the character and lifestyle of the people of the Kingdom of
          Heaven in a hostile world opposed to God's righteousness.

Jesus' Cluster of Christian Characteristics and Virtues

5:3 – Poverty of spirit – Intellectual response to life without God
5:4 – Grief of spirit – Emotional response to spiritual poverty
5:5 – Submission of spirit – Volitional response to spiritual need
5:6 – "Hungry and Thirsty" after righteousness – Motivational response for
          God's righteousness
5:7 – Merciful (forgiving) spirit and attitude – Relational response toward people
5:8 – Purity of heart – Vertical spiritual response toward God and God toward us
5:9 – Peaceful heart and reconciliation – Horizontal response in relationships
5:10,11 – Persecution willingness for righteousness sake –Sacrificial response
5:12 – Jubilant heart – Dispositional response for an eternal reward.

B. *Romans 12:9-21* (*vv 9-16* Christian Love within the church; *vv 17-21* Christian love
          within /outside the church.)
      Author: Paul who wrote letters to 7 Gentile churches
      Date: 56-58 AD? Third Missionary Journey
      Place of Writing: Corinth in the home of Gaius – *Rom 16:23*
      Major Theme: Justification by faith

Purpose: Appeal for prayer support – *Rom 15:30-32*; Announce plans to visit
Christians in Rome and deal with internal problems; launch a ministry in
Spain – *Rom 15:24*
Secretary: Tertius *Rom 16:22*
Carrier: Phebe *Rom 16:1*

Problems: Categories of Christian groups within the church at Rome which
contributed to internal problems.
1) Jewish Christians – abandoned Old Testament traditions and became
Orthodox New Testament Christians
2) Jewish Christians – retained Old Testament traditions (Judaizers)
3) Gentile Christians – came from pagan background (may have looked
down on Jewish Christians)
4) Gentile Christians – who were Jewish proselytes observing Jewish
traditions
5) Gentile Christians who filled a leadership vacuum during Jewish
excommunication from Rome 49-54 AD; Jewish Christian's return to
Rome to encounter Gentile leadership.

Romans 12:9-16
Paul begins this moral and ethical section on Christian living with the concept of
Divine Love. From this powerful moral force come all of the following derivatives of a
Christian lifestyle.

12:9 – Love (Divine) without hypocrisy
Abhor evil
Cleave to good
55 commands in the Bible to love
16 commands to love one another
9 commands to love your neighbor as yourself
2 commands to love one another fervently
12:10 –
Be kindly affectionate toward one another
Be devoted to one another in brotherly love NASB
Be respectful of one another
Be esteeming others better than self
12:11 –
Be diligent (in God's work)
Be aglow with the Spirit – RSV
Be a bond slave for the Lord
12:12 –
Be rejoicing in hope
Be patient in tribulation
Be persistent in prayer – GSPD
12:13 –
Be generous and hospitable
12:14 –
Be a blesser and not a cursor of those who persecute you
12:15 –
Be happy with those who are happy
Be sad with those who are sad
(Be empathetic)

12:16 –
   Be harmonious
   Be not proud or haughty
   Be respectful
   Be adaptable to people of low position
   Be humble – not conceited
12:17 –
   Be non-revengeful
   Be honorable, honest, noble, above reproach
12:18 –
   Be a peace maker
12:19 –
   Be non-revengeful
   Be respectful of God's justice
12:20 –
   Be better than your enemy
   Be sensitive to his need and respond appropriately
12:21 –
   Be victorious over evil with good.

C. *I Corinthians 13:1-8*
   Author: Paul
   Date: 55 or 56 AD
   Place of Writing: Ephesus – after spending 18 months in Corinth;
      3rd missionary journey
   Purpose: To address problems in the Church; address some questions from the
      Church; announce plans to visit the Church.
   Problems:
      Pride
      Rebellion against Apostolic authority
      Resorting to civil courts to resolve church matters
      Abuse of gifts, Christian liberties
      Carnality/Immaturity
      Tongues issue
      Immorality
      Contentious spirit
      Envy
      Lack of support for Christian workers
      Lack of understanding of the Holy Spirit
      Lack of discipline
      Lack of love

Because of the numerous problems within the church, Paul challenges the church to focus their attention on the greatest moral force within the Universe, namely, divine love (agape).

This is the kind of love Christ taught in His ministry, and demonstrated on the Cross. This kind of love is imparted to every born again believer who is truly consecrated to the Lordship of Christ. *Jn 13:35, 15:12*

Please note the following characteristics of true Christian love as divided into four categories of spiritual virtues.

<u>What it is</u> – *13:4a*
    Patient
    Kind

<u>What it is not</u> – *13:4b-5*
    Envious
    Boastful
    Arrogant
    Rude
    Selfish
    Touchy
    Suspicious
    Unforgiving

<u>What it rejoices in</u> – 13:6
    Rejoices in the truth – not people's failures

<u>What it does</u> – *13:7*
    Protects
    Trusts
    Hopes
    Endures

D. *Galatians 5:13-26*
    Author: Paul
    Date: 48? 49? (55-56?)   First Pauline Epistle?
    Place of Writing: Antioch
    Location of Churches: Galatia is in modern Turkey. Most likely those churches
        established by Paul and Barnabas on the first missionary journey – Pisidia,
        Antioch, Iconium, Lystra, Derbe
    Unique Features: Called an outline for the book of Romans to be written 10 years
        later.
    Letter of Contrast: Flesh vs Spirit; World vs Cross; Faith vs Law;
        Circumcision vs New Creation.
    Paul's Theology: Grace + Faith + Love + Spirit = Righteousness and keeping of
        Ethical Law
    Purpose: Refute the work of the Judaizers and Libertines
    Problems: Paul's Apostlic credentials questioned.
        Judaizers teaching Gentiles must become Jews by circumcision before they
            could become Christians.
        Both Jewish and Gentile Christians must keep the Mosaic Laws, regulations,
            and ceremonies.
        Libertines – Freedom from legalistic bondage and an emphasis on the Spirit
            which gives freedom to "do as you please."

Paul's attempt to disarm and resolve the problems among the Galatian Christians
focused on the contrast between the traits of the "flesh" versus the traits of the
"Spirit." Gal 5:13-26.

The cluster of Christian virtues is presented in the context of the *"Fruit of the Spirit"* *Gal 5:22-23.*

Please note that this list of virtues commences with (Divine) love out of which comes the derivatives of Divine love within a Spirit-filled and controlled life. They are arranged in a triad of traits.

Love	Longsuffering (patience)	Faith (faithfulness)
Joy	Gentleness (kindness)	Meekness (humility)
Peace	Goodness (generosity)	Temperance (Self-control)

E. *Ephesians 4:25-32, 5:1-5*
    Author: Paul
    Date: 60 AD (62 AD)?
    Place of Writing: Rome – Prison
    Major Theme: Mystery of Christ and His Church
    Location of Church(es): Circular letter sent to various churches starting at Ephesus?
    Purpose: To teach believers of their riches in Christ,
        To teach that the Church is the Building, Body, and Bride of Christ,
        To teach believers holiness of heart and a Christian lifestyle, and
        To equip believers for spiritual warfare.
    Problems: Most likely multicultural church tensions between Gentiles and Jews.
        Note the emphasis on unity and togetherness within the body of Christ.
        Apparently there were elements of dishonesty, hostility, verbal attack, and
        moral impurity.

Paul presents a basic moral and ethical lifestyle which compliments God's blueprint by which we were designed. These spiritual virtues enable us to function at our best and honor the blessings of God upon our life.

Every Christian, who represents these godly characteristics, will contribute to the unity of the Body of Christ, and live a life of God's true righteousness and holiness. *Eph 4:24*

    4:25 – Be honest – not deceptive
    4:26 – Be angry – but don't sin
    4:27 – Be vigilant – don't open doors for the devil
    4:28 – Be a giver – not a taker
    4:29 – Be a blesser – not a curser
    4:30 – Be Spirit sensitive – not Spirit insensitive
    4:31 – Be emotionally and spiritually clean – not loaded with emotional and
        spiritual garbage.
    4:32 – Be kind – not harsh
        Be tender hearted – not indifferent
        Be forgiving – not unforgiving
    5:1 – Be imitators of God – not imitators of the flesh
    5:2 – Be love motivated – not self-serving
    5:3-5 –Be morally pure – not immoral

F. *Philippians 4:4-9, 11, 13, 19*
      Author: Paul
      Date: 62 AD?
      Place of Writing: Most likely Rome while in prison
      Major Theme: Joy in Christ
      Purpose: Thanksgiving for the Church's financial gift
            Update on condition of their choice member –Epaphroditus
            Desire to send Timothy to minister to them
            Address problems within the church
            Encouragement and instructions on dealing with problems
      Problems:
            Perplexity over the health of Epaphroditus
            Poverty
            Pervasion of heresy within the church
            Persecution
            Personality conflict between 2 women *Phil 4:2-3*

The Philippian Epistle (Epistle of Joy) was written by a "problematic Apostle," who had problems in the past, problems in the now, and was facing major problems in the future. "How could Paul write such a positive letter to a problematic church?" An attempt to answer this question is made in *Chapter 6.*

In the meantime, read Philippians *4:4-8, 11, 13, 19,* and carefully observe Paul's listing of Christian virtues by which we are to live in a problematic world--spiritual virtues that enable us to be victorious in the midst of life's problems.

Reflect on these virtues in the context of a spiritual focus. This is a key to a better understanding of these verses. And remember Paul's personal declarations in *Philippians 3:13-14 "…this one thing I do, forgetting those things which are behind, and reaching forth unto those things which are before, I press toward the mark for the prize of the high calling of God in Christ Jesus."*

Paul's focus was not on the problems of the past, but rather on his future potential in Christ.

        4:4 – Focus on praise – not lament
        4:5 – Focus on poise – not on instability
        4:5 – Focus on the presence of God – not on aloneness
        4:6 – Focus on prayer and thanksgiving – not on worry or ingratitude
        4:7 – Focus on peace – not on conflict
        4:8 – Focus on the positive – not on the negative
        4:11 – Focus on patience – not on impatience
        4:13 – Focus on power – not on weakness *II Tim 1:7*
        4:19 – Focus on provision – not on want

G. *Colossians 3:1-17*
      Establishment of Church: founded by Epaphras and Philemon
      Author: Paul
      Date: 60/61 AD
      Place of Writing: Roman imprisonment under house arrest *Acts 28:30*

Major Theme: Absolute supremacy and sufficiency of Christ as Head of Creation
and the Church
Purpose: To refute heretical inroads
To teach Christ is supreme over all
To encourage holiness of heart and a holy lifestyle
Problems: Strange mixture of false Greek philosophy and Judaistic legalism and
ceremonialism

Greek Philosophical and Religious Heresy
Superior knowledge is key to salvation
Worship of many gods
Worship of angels
Christ was an angelic creature (a higher emanation)
Denial of Christ's humanity/deity
Denial of Christ's sufficiency for salvation

Judaistic Legalism and Ceremonialism
Salvation is:
Christ plus Jewish ceremonialism
Christ plus circumcision
Christ plus dietary laws and Holy days
Christ plus asceticism – absence of any form of natural pleasure

Give special attention to *Colossians 3:12-16*. Observe the spiritual virtues listed and
shared by Paul with the Colossian Church.

3:12 – bowels of mercies – tenderness, compassion
3:12 – kindness
3:12 – humbleness of mind – humility
3:12 – meekness – gentleness
3:12 – Longsuffering – patience
3:13 – Forbearing one another
3:13 – Forgiveness
3:14 – Love
3:15 – Peace
3:16 – Words of Christ within (Biblical thinking)

H. *I Thessalonians 5:16-24*
Author: Paul
Date: 50/51 AD Second Missionary Trip
Place of Writing: Corinth
Purpose: To compliment and encourage the Christians and address certain
problems
Problems:
Persecution
Slander against Paul's ministry
Rebuke for laxness
Rebuke for sexual immorality
Relieve concern about deceased Christians before Christ's return
Reassurance of Christ's return
Need to work

Need to respect leadership
Need for harmony, happiness, holy habits, and holy living
Need to allow for spiritual gifts
Need to respect the Spirit's movings.

In *Thessalonians 5:16*-24, Paul lists 10 Christian virtues that identify the spiritually mature and healthy Christian and church, and compliments the Divine blueprint by which we were designed.

5:16 – Be Joyful – not joyless
5:17 – Be Prayerful – not worried
5:18 – Be Thankful – not ungrateful
5:19 – Be Sensitive to the Spirit – not insensitive
5:20 – Be Respectful of prophesying (preaching) – not disrespectful
5:21 – Be Scrutinizing "prove all things" – not gullible
5:21 – Be Obedient – cling to truth- not disobedient
5:22 – Be Disciplined "abstain from all evil" – not undisciplined
5:23a – Be Holy – not unholy
5:23b – Be Hopeful of Christ's return – not hopeless

I. *II Peter 1:4-8*
    Author: Peter
    Date: 64-67 AD?
    Place of Writing: Probably in a Roman prison just prior to his death
    Written to all Christians throughout Northern Galatia
    Purpose:
        To challenge Christians to *"grow in the grace and knowledge of our Lord and Savior Jesus Christ" II Pt 3:18 RV*
        To remind Christians of God's provision for salvation and spiritual maturity
        To assure Christians of Christ's return
    Problems:
        Concern over spiritual immaturity, indifference and stagnation,
        Concern over false teachers and dangers of apostasy entering the church,
        Concern over inroads of scoffers (a heresy) who mock Christ's return.

The following list of Christian virtues is known as the 7 graces of Christian living. The emphasis is placed on the spiritual growth of each characteristic.

1:5 – Grow in moral virtue – excellence, character power, energy
        Emphasis on our "spiritual heart"
1:5 – Grow in spiritual knowledge – Biblical knowledge
        Emphasis on our mind
1:6 – Grow in temperance – self discipline
        Emphasis on our body
1:6 – Grow in patience – perseverance
        Emphasis on our will
1:6 – Grow in godliness – holy habits
        Emphasis on our spirit
1:7 – Grow in brotherly kindness
        Emphasis on our friendships
1:7 – Grow in Divine love *(agapeo)*
        Emphasis on our enemies

You are encouraged to review each of the above clusters of Christian virtues. It is recommended that you take a sheet of paper and write down each moral virtue, starting with *Mt 5:3-12* and continue through *II Pt 1:5-7.*

Now prayerfully evaluate your own Christian character in the context of this list and allow the Lord to speak to you through this spiritual exercise.

Chapter 6

The Problematic World in Which We Live and the Christian's New Perspective on Problems

We live in a problematic world that subjects us to various kinds of physical, mental, emotional, social, spiritual, financial, environmental, and political problems. This reality is influenced and impacted by 5 distinct negative moral forces.

Five Negative Moral Forces which challenges our moral life.

1. The Curse of Sin, both upon the earth and all of mankind, resulting from man's disobedience in the Garden of Eden. *Gen 3:16-19; Rom 8:19-23*

2. The Demonic Kingdom of Darkness and Evil, orchestrated by an "evil being," Satan himself. *Eph 6:10-18; I Pt 5:8-9*

   This invisible evil kingdom consists of tiers of evil spirits as categorized by the Apostle Paul in *Ephesians 6:12, "For we wrestle not against flesh and blood, but:*

   -against principalities – leaders among the demons who serve Satan. Demonic rulers over large areas, such as nations.

   -against powers – evil spirits under the authority of principalities – territorial spirits.

   -against the rulers of the darkness of this world – evil spirits in authority over this world.

   -against spiritual wickedness in high places – spiritual agents from the very headquarters of evil. (Phillips) This may refer to the character of the evil spirits in each of the above categories, and the evil spirits in our atmosphere.

   There is also another invisible kingdom, known as the Kingdom of Heaven (Righteousness or God). This Kingdom was brought into reality through the written Word of God (the Bible), through Christ the Living Word of God, through the out-pouring of the Spirit of God on the Day of Pentecost, and through the establishment of the Church of God, the Body of Christ, also on the Day of Pentecost. *Acts 2:1-4*

   Because of these two opposing Kingdoms, every moral being is caught in a cosmic battle. There is the continual tension between these two opposing kingdoms and the moral forces they represent. Consequently, every person in particular, and every society in general must morally choose between the following characteristics they represent.

Kingdom of Darkness		Kingdom of God, Righteousness, and Heaven
(Death)		(Life)
Deception	vs	Truth
Ungodliness	vs	Godliness
Unrighteousness	vs	Righteousness
Flesh	vs	Spirit
Sin	vs	Holiness of God
Conflict	vs	Peace
Hatred	vs	Love
Injustice	vs	Justice
Doubt	vs	Faith
Despair	vs	Hope
Evil	vs	Good
Earthly	vs	Heavenly

3. The Worldly System of secular institutions, teachings of false values, secular philosophies, distorted thinking, and fleshly lifestyles. The "world" in this context, is any person, possession, pleasure, or philosophy that redirects our focus from God to the *"lust of the flesh, lust of the eyes, and the pride of life." I Jn 2:15-17*

4. The Spiritual "Flesh" (sarx), and its "sin principle," within the spiritual heart, and the Physical Flesh (soma), and its weaknesses, and our susceptibility to temptation. It is to be noted that the Greek word *sarx* is sometimes used to refer to the natural body, without any connection to the moral principle of sin.

5. The Dysfunctional and Unhealthy People in families and society – Some people are very toxic in their personalities and may be morally depraved. They project their dysfunction and victimize their families and others with whom they interact. Examples include the extreme neurotics, sociopaths, and character disorder personalities, etc.

    These negative forces give rise to 8 categories of problematic sources.

Eight Sources of Problems

    Every problem we encounter comes from one or more of the following sources.

1. Self-imposed – Lifestyle, bad choices, accidents due to carelessness, etc.

2. Other people imposed – Lifestyle choices, anger, negligence, deception, revenge, etc. Generational sins *Ex 20:5*

3. Politically and Economically imposed – Dictatorship, corruption, war, slavery, etc.

4. Philosophically and theologically imposed – Secular humanism, liberal philosophies, relativism, etc., which negates Divine Authority and moral absolutes, and contributes to distorted views of God and life, idolatry, etc. (Worldly systems).

5. Environmentally imposed – Weather, pollution, earthquakes, floods, volcanic eruptions, etc.

6. Demonically imposed – E.g. *Job; Eph 6:10-18*

7. Divinely imposed – Divine judgments, curses, plagues, etc. brought about by spiritual disobedience, idolatry, rebellion, moral corruption, oppression, etc. (e.g. Egyptian plagues, Jonah's storm on the sea, etc.) .

8. Sin's Curse imposed – The Bible declares that the curse of sin is upon all nature and life, causing death, disease, dying, major upheaval, and dysfunctions of all kinds, such as mechanical, etc. *Gen 3:14-19; Rom 8:22-23*

The curse of sin greatly impacts all dimensions of our total being. <u>Our body</u> is constantly susceptible to sickness, infirmities, aging, and death. It is fragile and greatly restricted by limitations of space, strength, speech, and weariness.

<u>Our mind</u> is limited by its ability to always think clearly, remember, and exercise wise judgement.

<u>Our emotions</u> are sometimes unpredictable and subject to significant "highs" and "lows," positive and negative feelings, etc.

<u>Our social skills</u> are sometimes inadequate, awkward, and inappropriate, thus causing interpersonal conflict and alienation.

<u>Our spiritual life</u> is subject to sin, temptation, major moral failure, and guilt.

The Bible also states that specific curse(s) are brought upon individual families, societies, and nations because of idolatry, rebellion, pride, and a flagrant violation of divine laws and principles. *Ex 20:15; Deut 11:26-28, 28:15-68*

No matter how godly we may be, our Christian faith will not exempt us from problems. In fact, the more we are committed to Christ, the more we invite attack from the Demonic Kingdom, the Worldly System, and the heart of "fleshly" minded people. We see this referenced in the scriptures.

The Psalmist said, *"Many are the afflictions (troubles) of the righteous, but the Lord delivereth him out of them all." Ps 34:19*

The Apostle Paul stated, *"we are perplexed on every side, but not in despair, persecuted, but not forsaken, cast down (struck down), but not destroyed." II Cor 4:8*

Paul reminded Timothy, *"…all that will live godly in Christ Jesus shall suffer persecution." II Tim 3:12*

But the Word of God clearly teaches that none need to fail. The repeated theme of the scripture is that provision has been made for all to possess and live a life of spiritual strength, courage, triumph, and victory in this problematic world.

It should be the goal of every Christian to say with the Apostle Paul, *"I can do all things through Christ which strengthens me." Phil 4:13,* and *"we are more than conquerors through him that loved us, for I am persuaded that (nothing)…shall be able to separate us from the love of God…" Rom 8:37-39*

But, this kind of victory comes only to those who are ever on spiritual guard, exercise spiritual disciplines, and avail themselves of the spiritual resources God has provided for His people.

A. The Christian's View, Attitude, and Response to Problems

Someone has correctly said, "There are two kinds of people – those who have problems and those who are about to have problems." There is ample support for this statement, inasmuch, as we all live in a problem-centered world. Consequently, we learned a particular coping style and approach to the problems that come our way. Our natural response is highly contingent on our:

1. Temperament – Some people are by nature more hysterical, excitable, impulsive, and reactionary to life's adversities. The New Testament characters, Peter and Martha, reflect this temperament type. Others respond with greater patience, poise, and thoughtfulness. Mary, a sister to Lazarus certainly fits this temperament type.

2. Thinking style and insights– Each person has his or her own thinking style. Some are inclined to be impulsive, some calculated, some pessimistic, while others view life from a more optimistic perspective. No matter our thinking style, we will always perceive, evaluate, and interpret a problematic situation in the context of our:
    Level of knowledge about the situation,
    Level of personal resources and powers over the situation,
    Level of our perceived threat the situation presents, and the
    Level of faith, or lack thereof, in a Divine power greater than the situation.

3. Environmental Background – Children tend to model the behavior of their parents. Some families are crisis sensitive. Any adverse situation throws the whole family into an uproar. Family members may become hostile and distance themselves from each other. Other families approach problems in a more mature manner. They will draw closer and find security in each other's love and support.

4. Emotional Stability and Moods – Some people are more prone to mood swings.

5. Maturity Level – Maturity reflects a rational and reasonable approach toward life. Immaturity is characterized with more of an infantile response to life's challenges, such as self-centeredness, impatience, impulsivity, and explosive behavior.

6. Physiology – Hormonal levels, weariness, hunger, health, etc.

7. Spiritual Resources, Insights and Maturity
      Faith
      Prayer
      Promises of God
      Spiritual examples
      Support from the body of Christ

Carefully examine your current response and attitude toward problems, and provide an answer to the following questions:
Has my faith in Christ made a difference in my attitude and response to problems? Have I really tried to learn a healthier and more appropriate response to life's problems based on Biblical teachings and thinking, ministries of the Holy Spirit, and faith in the power and providence of God?

The Bible gives Christians a well-defined biblical perspective on problems. It teaches that our conflicts and frustrations are to be viewed unlike that of the secular mind. However, many Christians do not distinguish themselves from the average non-believer when it comes to coping with conflicts and problems. They are viewed as problem-centered and project a strong negative reaction toward adversity. They dwell on their problems and find meaning in life with a problem orientation. Some assume a victim's role and will often use their problems as a means to excuse themselves from responsibilities and new pursuits of life. They are governed by fear, worry, pessimism, doubt and self-pity. They attempt to cope through forms of "acceptable" addictions such as: food, prescribed medication, sleep, excessive T.V. viewing, etc.

But God through His Word teaches a better view and approach toward life's problems. The Bible cites many examples of individuals struggling with and responding to problems. A study of the following scriptures and Biblical characters should challenge the sincere Christian to evaluate their own response to problems, and be motivated toward a more spiritually mature approach.

Joseph's response to life's rejections and injustices is a challenge to all who read his life's story. (Gen 37-50).
-His brothers betrayed him and sold him into slavery.
-The slave merchants took him to Egypt and sold him to Potiphar, one of Pharoah's
      top officials.
-Potipher's wife falsely accused him of sexual impropriety resulting in his
      imprisonment. In spite of these horrendous sins against him, he never
      assumed a negative attitude, or turned against God. Consequently, God
      blessed him and propelled him to the second highest position in the Egyptian
      government.
-Joseph's brothers were compelled to travel to Egypt for grain. Because of a famine
      and through a series of events, they ultimately came in contact with Joseph.
-This encounter caused them to suffer tremendous regret and guilt.
-Joseph's attitude toward his brothers and the problems they caused him was…"ye
      thought evil against me; but God meant it unto good…" Gen 50:20
-Joseph saw his problem in the context of God's providence.

After several calamities in Job's life the Bible says, *"…Job got up and tore his robe and shaved his head. Then he fell to the ground in worship and said…May the name of the Lord be praised." NIV Job 1:20-22, 19:25-26*

The prophet Elisha and his servant were in Dothan surrounded by the armies of King Aram. The order was given to capture Elisha, because he had the God-given ability to discern the king's plans against Israel, and share them with Israel's king.

When Elisha's servant awakened and saw the City of Dothan encircled by Aram's army, he was greatly troubled and asked Elisha, *"…what shall we do?"* Elisha's response was *"Those who are with us are more than those who are with them."* Then he prayed, *"O Lord, open his eyes so he may see."* Immediately the servant's eyes were opened to the spiritual world around them. He saw the supernatural armies of God encircling him and Elisha. *II Kgs 6:15-17 NIV*

This lesson teaches that the greater our faith and walk with God, the greater our spiritual insights and poise in the midst of life's adversities. Jesus taught that our faith in God should always supersede the "fears" and "worries" that storms can bring into our life. He taught that we are to keep the eternal perspective in mind when confronted with life's battles.

Jesus said we are to *"rejoice, and be exceeding glad, when persecuted and falsely accused for His sake."* Why? Because, *"great is our reward in heaven…" Mt 5:12*

He taught the disciples not to give in to worry over the essentials of life, for it is God who will care for those who trust in Him, and *"seek first his Kingdom, and his righteousness" Mt 6:33*

Christ rebuked Martha because of her anxious spirit over preparing a meal while He commended her sister, Mary, for her poise as she sat at the feet of Christ listening to His words of eternal life. *Lk 10:38-42*

The disciples were rebuked by Christ for their fear and lack of faith during a terrifying storm, while in a boat with Christ. Mk 4:35-41. This spiritual rebuke is meaningful when viewed in the context of Christ's:
   -Recent performance of great miracles in their presence.
   -Command to get into the boat and go with Him to the other side of the lake.
   -Presence with the disciples while on the boat, even though He had gone to
       sleep.

Faith is easy to possess when life has no major storms. But the real test of faith comes <u>during</u> the storms of life. It is the storms that will always challenge and reveal the depth and quality of our faith.

Prior to Christ's arrest and crucifixion, He reminded the disciples of His peace and power in a troubled world. Therefore, they should not be troubled, fearful, or disheartened, for He said:

"Peace I leave with you, my peace I give unto you: not as the world giveth, give I unto you. Let not your heart be troubled, neither let it be afraid." Jn 14:27

"These things I have spoken unto you, that in me ye might have peace. In the world ye shall have tribulation; but be of good cheer; I have (through my power) overcome the world." Jn 16:33; c.f. I Jn 5:4

The Apostle Peter experienced imprisonment and great opposition to his faith in Christ. But he admonished Christian's not to focus on life's problems, but rather on our *"lively hope"* of an *"incorruptible inheritance,"* and the perfecting of our faith, which is to bring rejoicing. *I Pt 1:3-8*

James admonished Christians to, *"Count it all joy when you fall into diver's (various kinds of) temptations." Jms 1:2* Why? Because God uses problems to put all of our spiritual "parts" together (entire) and mature (*teleios*) them within our Christian character.

But of all the New Testament writers, it is the Apostle Paul who gives us the greatest insight into the mature Christian's view and attitude toward problems. Throughout his entire Christian life he knew what it was to experience persecution, multiple perils, and various kinds of problems. *II Cor 4:7-12, 11:23-33* He made it known throughout his New Testament writings that he suffered from:

Afflictions
Arrests by the Romans
Assassination attempts on his life

Beatings with rods three times
Beatings with whips five times, with 39 stripes each time totaling 195 stripes
Burdens for the churches

Chains of a prisoner
Coldness
Criticism

Deaths often
Distress

Evil reports
Eye problems? – *Gal 4:15*

Fastings often
Feet placed in stocks

Grief

Hunger/Thirst

Imprisonment four times
Infirmities

Jealousy from others
Journeys often with many perils

Lack of money

Mockings
Misrepresentation

Nakedness (Lack of adequate clothing.)

Perils of countrymen, robbers, opponents, water, wilderness, sea
Persecution

Rejection from both friends and enemies
Reproach

Shipwreck three times
Sleeplessness
Snake bite
Sorrows of various kinds
Stoned with rocks (Lystra)
Storms on the sea

Thorn in the flesh
Tribulations

Weariness
Wild beasts

Yet Paul's attitude and approach toward problems is both challenging and insightful. To the Roman Church he said, *"And we know that all things work together for good to them that love God, to them who are the called according to his purpose. For whom he did foreknow, he also did predestinate to be conformed to the image of his son…"* Rom 8:28-29

"…if God be for us, who can be against us?" Rom 8:31

"Who shall separate us from the love of Christ?" Rom 8:35

"Nay, in all these things we are more than conquerors (victors) through him that loved us." Rom 8:37

To the Corinthian Church he declared, *"As sorrowful, yet always rejoicing…"* I Cor 6:10

To the Thessalonian Church he emphatically stated that we should:
"Rejoice evermore" I Thess 5:16
"Pray without ceasing" I Thess 5:17
"In everything give thanks…" I Thess 5:18

Paul's Philippian Epistle gives the greatest insight into the Christian's approach to problems. He was in prison (most likely in Rome) facing a very problematic situation. His future was uncertain as he faced possible execution. His critics were attacking him and his ministry. Then, there was the concern over the Philippian Church, who he, Silas, Timothy and Luke established on his second missionary journey. The church was confronted with:

Persecution

Poverty

Pervasion of heresy, and

Perplexity over the health of Epaphroditus, a choice member of the church, who had become seriously ill on his journey to visit Paul with a gift from the church. There was also concern over two contentious women within the church. *Phil 4:2-3*

In spite of all the problems he had encountered, was encountering, and would encounter in the future, Paul wrote the Philippian letter (Epistle of Joy) to a problematic church.

It was in this Epistle that Paul assured the church that God was still in charge and they should conduct themselves in the context of this spiritual reality, and Paul's example of Christian faith. *Phil 4:9*

Paul admonished the church to:

1:6 – Be confident that God would complete the good work He started within them and the church.

1:12 – Be assured that the gospel was being advanced through Paul's imprisonment.

1:21 – Be assured of Paul's commitment to Christ and thus they too should be so committed.

1:27 – Be good examples of the gospel.

1:28 – Be courageous and not "terrified by their adversaries."

2:3 – Be non-contentious, but supportive of each other.

2:5 – Be humble even as Christ.

2:13 – Be aware of God's providence at work within their lives and the church.

2:14-15 – Be without "murmurings and disputings" so as to be good witnesses.

3:13-14 – Be focused on the future and not the past.

3:20 – Be ever conscious of their eternal citizenship in heaven and of Christ's return.

4:4 – Be joyful in the Lord.

4:5 – Be poised in their reactions to adversity with the knowledge that Christ is with them, and will return.

4:6 – Be prayerful, thankful, and not worried.

4:8 – Be refining in their thinking with good and positive thoughts.

4:11 – Be learning contentment even as Paul

4:13 – Be strong in the Lord even as Paul.

4:19 – Be assured of God's provision for them.

Paul's Christian faith never wavered because of the battles of life. In fact, prior to his death, he was able to write these words to Timothy:
"I have fought a good fight,
I have finished my course (race),
I have kept the faith." II Tim 4:7

It is only natural to ask, "What were the characteristics of Paul's dynamic Christian life that enabled him to withstand multiple perils of life and still be able to end his life's journey with great victory and triumph?"

Aside from his phenomenal encounter with Christ and spiritual transformation *(Acts 9:3-19),* the following spiritual traits characterize Paul's life and journey with Christ.

1. Alive in Christ – *Cor 5:17; Col 13:1*

2. Attitude of optimism in Christ – *Phil 2:13-15, 4:8; II Cor 6:10*

3. Ability to adjust and adapt to circumstances of which he had no control – *Phil 4:11*

4. Biblical thinking - *Rom 12:2; II Cor 10:5; Eph 4:23; Phil 4:8; Col 3:2, 10, 16*
   His fine-tuned Biblical thinking allowed him to see all of life in the context of God's:
   Providence – *Rom 8:28-29; Phil 1:6, 12, 2:13; Acts 16:7-11*
   Plan of Redemption – *Eph 1:4-22, 2:8-9; Col 1:9-14; Titus 2:11-14; Col 1:9-14*
   Purpose for him – *Eph 1:1, 2:10; Phil 2:13*
   Prayer benefits – *Eph 6:18; Phil 4:6-7*
   Peace – *Phil 4:6-7, 9; I Thess 5:23*
   Power – *Eph 3:20, 6:10; Phil 4:19; II Tim 1:7*
   Provision – *Phil 4:19*
   Promises – *Rom 15:4*
   Protection – *Rom 8:31*

5. Commitment and consecration to Christ, his Divine call, and the Gospel – *Rom 12:1; Gal 2:20; Phil 1:21, 3:10-11; Rom 1:16-17*

6. Discipline and determination centered around Christ and the call of God upon his life – *I Cor 2:2, 9:27; Phil 3:13-14*

7. Emotional and spiritual cleansing – *Eph 4:31; Col 3:8-9*

8. Faith – He referred to faith or believe 153 times – *Rom 1:17, 4:20-21, 5:1, 10:17, 14:23; Eph 2:8, 6:16.*

9. Grace of God upon his life – refers to grace 84 times – *Eph 2:8; Titus 2:11*. Grace appears in the salutation and conclusion of each of his letters. Paul's reference to grace refers to all God has done for us, of which we did not earn or deserve. It is also God's promised provision for all we might face or need in life, such as God's glory, resources, anointing, care, and empowerment. *II Cor 12:9; II Tim 2:1*

10. Gratitude and thanksgiving – refers to thanksgiving 30 times. *Phil 4:6; I Thess 5:18*

11. Harmony in relationships pursued – *Rom 12:18; Phil 2:1-4*. Paul presents the Gospel as a *"one another gospel,"* and the need for love and unity within the *"Body of Christ." Eph 4:1-6*

12. Humility of spirit – *Rom 12:16; Phil 2:5; Col 3:12; I Cor 15:9*. He considered himself least of the Apostles.

13. Hope – referred to 35 times. – *Rom 5:4-5, 15:4; Titus 2:11-13.*

14. Infilling of the Spirit and Heart Purity – *Gal 5:16-26; Eph 4:30, 5:18; Rom 8:1-16; I Thess 5:19; II Cor 7:1; Eph 1:4, 4:24, 5:25-27; I Thess 3:13, 4:3-7; I Tim 1:5; I Pt 1:22*

15. Joyfulness and rejoicing in the Lord – *Rom 12:12; Phil 4:4; I Thess 5:16.*

16. Love (Divine and Brotherly Love) – referred to love 60 times – *Rom 12:9-10, 13:8, 10; Gal 5:13-15, 22-23; Eph 5:1-2; Col 3:14; I Cor 13; I Tim 1:5.*

17. Peace of God and Heart – referred to peace 40 times – *Phil 4:7-9; Col 3:15; I Thess 5:23*

18. Power, might, and strength through God – referred to 47 times – *Eph 3:20, 6:10; II Tim 1:7*

19. Purpose for which to live greater than self – *Phil 1:21, 3:10-11; Gal 2:20*

20. Prayer – referred to 50 times – *Rom 12:12; Eph 6:18; Phil 4:6; Col 4:2; I Thess 5:17*

21. Second coming of Christ, resurrection in Christ, and our future with Christ – *Rom 8:18; I Cor 2:9; II Cor 4:17; Phil 3:20-21; I Thess 4:16-18; I Cor 15:51-55.*

An overview of the above information should serve as a motivator to evaluate and adjust our Christian view and approach to problems with a greater compliance to Biblical principles. Has your faith in Christ made a difference in your approach to problems?

B. The Christian's View of God's Power to Convert Problems into Good.

God in His wisdom can take any problem and use it for our spiritual good and His glory. Listed below are some positives that can come out of the negatives of problems.

To teach us the true value and meaning of life, and to never take for granted our personal blessings. *Job 1:21* Problems can cause us to slow up and become introspective and reflective.

To refine our character – *Rom 5:2-5, 8:28-29; Jms 1:2-4; I Pt 5:10* – To become more like Christ. God is more interested in our character than our comfort. Remember, patience comes out of tribulation. Rom 5:3

To inspire and motivate us to accomplish some great work for God. Some of the greatest songs, poems, and books were inspired and written in the midst of great peril. (Paul's letters were written while going through great adversities.)

To expand and enrich our faith and hope. Problems stretch us to grow and mature in Christian character and Biblical understanding. Book of *Job.*

To draw us closer to God with greater dependency on God. *II Cor 12:8-10*

To discipline and chastise us for disobedience. *Heb 12:5-11.*

To demonstrate before others His power within that enables us to effectively deal with problems. *II Cor 12:9-10.*

To sensitize us to the sufferings of others, and thus become more empathetic. *Rom 12:15.*

To help us to keep in perspective the earthly and eternal things, and to visualize God's promise of eternal life where there is freedom from problems. *Phil 3:20-21; Rom 8:18; Rev 21:4.*

To enable us to share in some degree the sufferings of Christ. *I Pt 4:12-13; Phil 3:10-11.*

To convert our human weakness into God's powerful strength upon and within us. *II Cor 12:7-10.* Problems reveal our weakness and God's glory, and serves to perfect His power through our weaknesses.

To provide an opportunity for a Divine miracle. There are no miracles without problems. *Mt 17:20*

C. The Christian's Approach to Problems

   1. Problems and the Discipline of a Biblical Mind

Always <u>accentuate</u> the positive and minimize the negative in any problematic situation. *Phil 4:8*

"<u>*Bring*</u> *every thought into captivity unto the obedience of Christ.*" *II Cor 10:5*

<u>Cancel</u> out negative thoughts with faith thoughts (*Phil 4:13*) and cleanse your mind with the Word of God. *Eph 5:25-27.*

<u>Dwell</u> on God's Power and Promises, and not on the problems of life. Diminish problems by maximizing God's power and promises. *Eph 1:19.*

<u>Expand</u> your mind with Biblical truth and achieve Biblical thinking by which to perceive, evaluate, and interpret life's events according to God's:
    Providence – *Phil 1:6; Rom 8:28*
    Plan of Redemption for our soul, body and the world in which we live.
    Purpose(s) – *Jer 29:11; Eph 2:10; Phil 2:13*
    Prayer Plan – *Jer 33:3; Mt 6:6, 7:7, 11; Phil 4:6*
    Peace Plan – *Isa 26:1; Jn 14:27, 16:33*
    Principles – *Deut 11:26-27; Phil 4:9*
    Power Sources – *Acts 1:8; II Tim 1:7; Eph 1:19, 3:20; Phil 4:13*
    Provision – *Phil 4:19*
    Promises – *Rom 15:4; II Pt 1:4* (7,000 promises)
    Protection – *Ps 34:7*
    Preparation for our eternal future – *Jn 14:1-3; Rom 8:18; I Cor 2:9;*
       II Cor 4:17-18

<u>Fortify</u> and feed your faith and not your worries, through the Word of God. *Rom 10:17; Mt 17:20.*

<u>Give</u> thanks and praise continuously. *Ps 34:1; Acts 16:25; I Thess 5:18*

<u>Harbor</u> holy, happy, harmonious thoughts—not sad, depressing, worried thoughts. *Isa 26:3; Pro 23:7; Phil 4:8*

<u>Intercept</u> any negative word before it is spoken and replace it with a positive, faith-driven word. (Remember, words help create the world in which you live.) *Pro 18:21*

<u>Just</u> refuse to worry about the problem. *Phil 4:6; I Pt 5:7,* and join your thoughts with the thoughts of faith hope, optimism, praise, expectancy, and the promises of God's Word.

2. Problems and the Spiritual Steps Toward Resolution

Plan A

Acknowledge you have a problem(s) bigger than you and you need a power greater than you to resolve or cope with it. You dare not live in denial of reality.

Bring your problems to the Lord in the spirit of faith and prayer.
 Phil 4:6; Jms 5:16

Confess your pain, anxiety, insecurity, need and ask God for His Divine grace and intervention. *Jer 33:3; Mt 6:6, 7:7, 11; Phil 4:6*

Declare your position with God even as Job
 "Though he slay me, yet will I trust him" Job 13:14.
 "I will trust you Lord with my problem."

Embrace godly people of mature Christian faith, wisdom, and confidentially with whom you entrust your problem(s) and know that they want to be helpful. E.g. The Paralytic *Mt 9:2-7; Mk 2:1-12; Lk 5:17-26.*

Focus on God's providence, promises, and power, not on your problems. *Rom 15:4; II Pt 1:4.*

Give gratitude and praise to God for His help and blessings. *Phil 4:6; I Thess 5:18; Ps 34:1.* Paul/Silas in prison – *Acts 16:23-26.* Always find something for which to give thanks.

Hope in the Lord. Faith and hope go together. Hope is the belief that something good is about to happen. *Ps 42:5, 11, 43:5, 71:5, 14; Heb 11:1.*

Imagery practice. Meditate on *Ps 23*. Attempt to close your eyes and see the images portrayed in this Psalm.

Just relax in the Lord, by taking a deep breath and releasing your problems into His care through the spirit of faith, prayer, and praise. *Mt 11:28; Isa 40:31.*

Keep in mind scriptural directives in dealing with problems. *Phil 4:4-9, 11, 13, 19; Jms 1:2-3.*

Learn to refine your thinking according to *Isa 26:3; II Cor 10:5; Phil 4:8,* and refuse to worry.

Make "agape" love and Biblical principles your primary governing forces for problem resolution. *I Cor 13*

Plan B

Relax in the Lord – *Phil 4:11*
Find a place of serenity and be alone with God. Take a deep breath, *"and be still and know that 'He' is God." Ps 46:10*

Refine your thinking – *Isa 26:3; II Cor 10:5; Phil 4:8; Col 3:2*
The mind often exaggerates problems and will view them with excessive negativity from which comes needless:
      Fear
      Exaggerations
      Worries
      Anxieties
      Negativity
      Doubts
      Crossing bridges prior to arrival
Confront these internal reactions with powerful faith promises and a focus on God's:
      Grace – *Heb 4:16*
      Rest – *Mt 11:28*
      Abundance – *Jn 10:10; Eph 3:20*
      Care – *I Pt 5:7*
      Empowerment – *Isa 41:10; Eph 3:10, 6:10; II Tim 1:7; Phil 4:13*
      Knowledge of your problem – *Ps 139:1-18; Job 1, 2, 42*
Endeavor to compare your problem in the context of God's power who created such a vast universe.

Focus on God's greatness, and how vast the universe is based on recent astronomical discoveries.

Remember, we now know there are two trillion galaxies with each galaxy consisting of 300 to 400 billion stars. Try to view your problem from this perspective of God's greatness.

Focus on *Deut 20:4 "For the Lord your God is the One, who goes with you to fight for you, against your enemies to give you victory."*

Reflect and meditate upon *Psalm 23.*

Relax and practice spiritual imagery with each scriptural concept in this Psalm. Envision the concept and speak it out loud. For example:
      "The Lord is my Shepherd"
            (Take a deep breath and form the mental picture of the
            shepherd caring for his sheep.)
      "I shall not want."
            (Take a deep breath and envision the shepherd coming
            toward you to meet your greatest need(s).
      "He maketh me to lie down in green pastures."
            (Take a deep breath and pull into focus a warm and beautiful
            sunny day as you lie down in the midst of refreshing and
            beautiful grass.)

Continue to follow this procedure throughout the entire Psalm.

Acknowledge your pain, anxiety, insecurities, need, suffering, or grief. Remember this truism, "If you can't acknowledge or feel it, you can't be healed from it."

Acknowledge God in all your ways—the past, present, and future. *Pro 3:5-6* Try to see how God has and is working in your life through people, circumstances, open doors, gifts, protection, mercies, etc. Give Him thanks. *I Thess 5:19*

Cooperate with God's providence (His care, awareness, resources, empowerment, promises, provisions, and protection over your life). Remember, God will use your problem to teach you, refine your character, and complete His purpose for your life. *Rom 8:28*

Experience one day at a time – *Mt 6:25-34.* Problems often tempt us to cross bridges before we get to them. God has promised grace and help sufficient for all the days of our life, but we must live one day at a time, for we have no assurance of tomorrow. *Jms 4:13-14; II Cor 9:8; Ex 16:4, 12; Lam 3:22-23; Ps 34:9-10*

Don't forget the spiritual resources available to you:
> Spiritual protection over, around, and under you,
> Spiritual promises for you, 7000 plus promises in the Bible.
> Spiritual powers within you: Faith, Spirit, Word of God, Prayer, Name of Jesus, etc.

Don't forget that you are a temporary dweller here on earth being prepared in character to be a permanent dweller in the eternal Kingdom of Heaven.

Don't forget that God can take your problem to demonstrate His power through you, to develop your character within you, and provide an opportunity for a miracle through you, in you, and around you, for His glory.

Remember, time has its own healing component, and patience is a virtue.

Remember, your actions and reactions to problems will be forever etched within your mind, and in the minds of all who observe you.

Chapter 7

The Christian's Spiritual Resources for a Victorious Life

God is not aloof or insensitive to the problems we encounter. The Bible teaches that we have a great High Priest in Christ, who is *"…touched with the feelings of our infirmities…" Heb 4:15.*

God through His wisdom and grace has given all the necessary protection, promises, and powers for a victorious life over every problem we may encounter.

A. The Spiritual Protection of God Around You.
   Learn and envision in your mind the following forms of divine protection around you, under you, over you, and before you.

   The Armor of the Lord is upon you. *Eph 6:10-18*

   The Angel of the Lord *encampeth* round about you. *Ps 34:7, 91:11*

   The Hedge (fence) of the Lord encircles you. *Job 1:10*

   The Lord stands beside you as a Mighty Warrior to help you. *Jer 20:11; Heb 13:6*

   The Shield and Buckler of the Lord's Truth is in front of you. *Ps 91:4*

   The Shield of the Lord's favor is over you. *Ps 5:12*

   The Songs of Deliverance are all around you. *Ps 32:7*

   The Everlasting Arms of the Lord are underneath you. *Deut 33:27*

   The Weapons formed against you will not prosper. *Isa 54:17*

   The Lord is within you, and *"greater is he that is in you than he that is in the world."* *I Jn 4:4*

   The Lord is for you and *"if God be for us, who can be against us." Rom 8:31*

   The Lord's Refuge is available to you, for *"He is our hiding place." Deut 33:27; Ps 32:7, 91:1-4.*

B. The Spiritual Promises of God for you. *II Pt 1:3-4; Rom 15:4*

   The following Biblical promises are key commitments from God for the righteous to hold on to in the midst of life's problems and storms.

   Endeavor to learn the following promises and apply them by faith throughout the rest of your life's journey. If you will sincerely do so, God will:

   (Never) <u>Abandon</u> you for He hath said, *"I will never leave you, nor forsake you." Heb 13:5; Rom 8:35-38*

(Never) <u>Allow</u> more to come upon you than you can bear (handle) for He knows your tolerance level. *I Cor 10:13*

<u>Bless</u> you (the righteous) in spite of your problems. *Josh 1:8; Ps 1:1-3, 5:12; Mt 5:10-12; Jms 1:12*

<u>Care</u> for you if you *"cast your care upon him, for he cares for you." I Pt 5:7*

<u>Defend and Deliver</u> you from your enemies and will:
    Defeat them. *Deut 20:4; Ps 91:3; Isa 54:17*
    Put them under your feet. *II Sam 22:40; Ps 18:39*
    Make a footstool out of them. *Ps 110:1*

<u>Empower</u> you by giving you inner strength and power. *Isa 40:31, 41:15; Acts 1:8; Eph 3:20; Phil 4:13*

<u>Fight</u> for you. *Deut 20:4; Isa 54:17; Ex 14:14 "The Lord will fight for you; you need only to be still." (NIV)*

<u>Give</u> you:
    Grace sufficient for the problem. *II Cor 12:7-8*
    Peace. *Jn 14:27, 16:33; Phil 4:67*
    Rest – *Mt 11:28*
    Wisdom – *Jms 1:5*

<u>Hear</u> your prayer. *Jer 33:3; Mt 7:7; Phil 4:6-7; Jms 5:16*

<u>Help</u> you. *Isa 41:10; Heb 13:5-6*

<u>Intercede</u> for you. *Rom 8:27, 34*

<u>Keep</u> you, for the Lord is our keeper. *Ps 121:3-5.*

<u>Love</u> you with an everlasting love. *Jer 31:3.*

<u>Make</u> *"all things work together for good to them who love God…" Rom 8:28*

<u>Protect</u> you with different kinds of protection. *Ps 23:4-6, 34:7, 91:11; Isa 54:17; II Thess 3:3*

<u>Renew</u> your strength. *Isa 40:31*

<u>Reward</u> you in the life to come. *Mt 5:10-12; James 1:12*

<u>Sabotage</u> all weapons formed against you. *Isa 54:17*

<u>Travel</u> with you wherever you go. Deut 31:6; *Josh 1:9; Ps 121; Isa 43:1-3*

(Give you) <u>Victory</u> over life's problems and enemies. *Rom 8:31, 35-38; I Cor 15:57; I Jn 4:4, 5:4*

C. The Spiritual Powers Within You – *Eph 3:20; II Tim 1:7; I Jn 4:4*

II Sam 22:40; "For you have given me strength for the battle..."
(TLB); I Sam 30:6; Isa 40:31; Lk 24:49; Acts 1:8, 4:33; Rom 1:16; Eph 3:20,
6:10; Phil 4:13 II Tim 1:7

The New Testament Church was birthed and built through the
supernatural power of the:
> Resurrection *Eph 1:19,*
> Holy Spirit *Acts 1:8,* and the
> Gospel *Rom 1:16.*

The early disciples were empowered by various spiritual power sources
that enabled them to experience a tremendous transformation of life,
withstand persecution, and advance the Kingdom of God through the
church. They were so empowered by these sources that no adversity could
stop their vibrant faith and zeal for the Lord. As a result, miracles took
place, lives were remarkably transformed, and churches were established in the
midst of Roman opposition, pagan idolatry, and profane philosophies of the
day. This same kind of spiritual power is still available to all who seek it.

There are ten different spiritual power sources available to every born-again
believer. The listing of these power sources is an attempt to bring into focus
how much spiritual power Christians can possess in a problematic world.

1. Power of Faith
   Key Scriptures: *Pro 3:5-6; Heb 11:1-6; Hab 2:4; Rom 1:17; Gal 3:11;*
   Heb 10:38; Mt 8:13, 9:22, 29, 17:20, 19:26; Lk 1:37; Mk 9:23; Jn 20:29; Acts 6:5,
   8, 11:24, 15:9; Rom 1:17, 4:17, 20-21, 5:1, 10:17, 12:3, 14:23; II Cor 5:7;
   Gal 5:22-23; Eph 2:8-9, 6:16; I Pt 1:5; I Jn 5:4

   Faith is the primary key that releases God's power within our life. It enables
   God to work through our life to accomplish His purpose and will. It is that
   which connects us with the spiritual world. *II Kgs 6:17.* This power only
   comes from God and His Word.

2. Power of the Spirit - *Lk 24:49; Acts 1:8*
   The Spirit is that which gives spiritual life. The Spirit's power transforms,
   regenerates, and quickens our spirit. Total surrender to the will of God
   allows the Spirit to have greater power within us. *Acts 4:31, 33; Eph 5:18*

3. Power of the Word of God – *Pro 3:1-4, 4:20-23; Josh1:8; Ps 1:1-3;*
   Heb 4:12; Jn 15:7; II Tim 3:16-17
   The Word of God has tremendous power. It is God "inspired" and
   "breathed." We are to take the Word and renew our mind with Biblical
   truth, principles, promises, and allow it to generate faith within us.

4. Power of Biblical Thoughts that come out of a Transformed Heart and Renewed
   Mind *Rom 12:2; II Cor 5:17;*
   Read: *Pro 4:23, 23:7; Isa 26:3; II Cor 10:5; Phil 4:8*

The power of the Spirit brings about a transformed heart and mind. The natural mind, even though it has been greatly impaired by sin, also has tremendous innate power. We can assimilate over 17 trillion pieces of information by age 70. We can potentially think 50 thoughts per minute, 3000 thoughts per hour, and 72,000 thoughts per day.

Our thoughts impact every part of our being:
> Body – thoughts affect every cell of our body.
> Relationships
> Energy level
> Attitude
> Moods/emotions
> Spiritual life (faith)

When we are born again, the Spirit of God quickens the natural mind to bring about a transformed and renewed mind which is receptive to a new way of thinking and perceiving life. The transformed mind is renewed both by the Spirit and the Word. *II Cor 5:17* Our mind is to meditate on the Word of God, with the promise that it will bring forth great fruit and blessings. *Josh 1:8; Ps 1:1-3.*

The renewed mind can be greatly enriched by learning to perceive life and Biblical truth in the context of God's:
Providential actions in us and among us. *Rom 8:28*
Plan of redemption (His sacrifice, resurrection, Spirit, church, etc.)
Purpose for which we are to live life. *Jer 29:11; Phil 2:13*
Prayer response to our prayers. *Jer 33:3; Phil 4:6-7*
Peace. *Jn 14:27*
Principles and Laws by which to live. *Deut 11:26-28*
Power within our life. *Acts 1:8; Eph 3:20; Phil 4:13*
Provisions in life. *Phil 4:19*
Promises for our life. *II Pt 1:4; Rom 15:4*
Protection upon our life. *Ps 34:7*
Preparation for our earthly and heavenly future. *Jn 14:1-3*
Promised return of Christ. *I Cor 15:51-55; I Thess 4:13-18*

5. Power of Divine Love out of a Pure Heart *Jn 13:35, 15:12; Rom 5:1-5, 12:9-10; I Cor 13; I Tim 1:5*
    Total surrender to the Lordship of Christ, and a sincere prayer for total cleansing of the heart from the "principle of sin," or "the sin," brings about the "infilling of the Spirit," and the outflow of "agape" love.

    This kind of love is such a powerful motivating force that it is known as the greatest moral force within the Universe. *"There is nothing love cannot face."* (*I Cor 13:7 NEB*) It is that kind of love that enables the believer to:
    > Bless and not curse their enemies
    > Pray for their enemies
    > Forgive their enemies
    > Sacrifice for the cause of Christ
    > Suffer and die for Christ

Christian love had such an influence on the cruel Roman culture that it was not uncommon to hear these words, "O, how they love one another." (Tertullian) This moral force will always generate within us:

> Perseverance
> Unity
> Motivation
> Peace
> Edification
> Discipline
> Hope
> Optimism
> Praise
> Expectancy
> Sacrifice

6. Power of Words from a Spiritually Tamed and Trained Tongue
   Ps 19:14, 34:1, 141:3; Pro 6:2, 10:11, 12:18, 18:21; Mt 12:34, 36-37, 17:20; Mk 11:23; Eph 4:29; Col 4:6; Jms 3:1-12 – Something to ponder…
   How many words do you speak per day and how fast do you speak them?

The English language consists of about 800,000 words. The average person knows about 10,000 and will only use about 500 different words per day. We will always live in the context of our words and the words of others, and they become our reality. This author makes no claims to originality on this subject. However, through scriptural teaching and insights gleaned from others, it is apparent that words contain tremendous power. They represent multiple powers upon our life and others. Experts on this subject conclude that words contain:

> Relational Power – Words are relational and connective in nature. They have the power to connect or disconnect us with people. Love requires connective words in order to live and survive.
>
> Creative Power *Pro 18:21 "Death and life are in the power of the tongue…"*
> Even as God created the world with His words, so do our words have creative power. Our words can create:
>> Life or death
>> Love or hate
>> Blessing or cursing
>> Hope or despair
>> Optimism or pessimism
>> Excitement or indifference
>> Faith or doubt
>
> Magnetic Power
> Positive words tend to attract positive results and negative words tend to attract negative results.
>
> Predictive Power
> Our life, to some degree, will always move in the direction of our words. Positive words move us toward positive results, negative words toward negative results. Paul understood this principle when he wrote *"…whatsoever things are*

true…honest…just…pure…lovely…of good report…think on these things." Phil 4:8.

It is a given rule of life that we will speak words that reflect our thoughts. Always remember that positive thoughts produce positive words, and positive words provide positive results.

Spiritual and Eternal Power

Our words will impact the quality of our spiritual life. Also, words have eternity within them, for every word spoken lives on, and is recorded within our mind, the mind of others, and the mind of God. *Mt 12:36*

This very thought should challenge us to refrain from speaking recklessly and inappropriately. We will be wise to remember the words of the Psalmist, *"Set a watch, O Lord, before my mouth; keep the door of my lips." Ps 141:3*

There is tremendous benefit in learning to speak words of Biblical truth, blessings, affirmation, encouragement, hope, optimism, praise and thanksgiving. This is especially true whenever we put a Biblical truth into words, and declare it out loud. Our:

Thoughts will be focused on that Truth.
Heart will be filled with that Truth.
Faith will be increased by that Truth.
Spirit will be energized by that Truth.
Mouth will be inclined to repeat that Truth.

Remember, *"faith comes by hearing, and hearing by the Word of God." Rom 10:17*

The words of believers are even more powerful, when those words contain scripture, or a statement of Biblical truth, and are spoken out loud. *Mt 12:34*

It is suggested that the reader take one or more of the clusters of Christian virtues presented in Chapter 5, and apply this spiritual concept. For example, read and review I Thessalonians 5:16-23. Try to memorize each verse, and declare out loud your spiritual declaration.

Today, I will *"rejoice evermore."* v 16

Today, I will *"pray without ceasing."* v 17

Today, I will *"in everything give thanks…"* v 18

Today, I will honor and not *"quench the Spirit."* v 19

Today, I will respect and not despise *"prophesying"* (preaching) or the foretelling of Divine truth. v 20

Today, I will *"prove all things"* and not be gullible. v 21

Today, I will *"hold fast to that which is good."* v 21

Today, I will *"abstain from all appearance of evil."* v 22

Today, I will be *"sanctified wholly"* in spirit, soul, and body. v 23

Today, I will *"be preserved blameless unto the coming of our Lord Jesus Christ."* v 23

A list of "I Am's", "I Will's", and "I Will Not's" in Christ are also provided to illustrate and put into practice these truths. (Addendums III, IV, & V).

These thoughts are placed in alphabetical order for easy memorization. Speak out loud these lists, and make them a part of your daily spiritual discipline. Remember, Christ's miracles were normally preceded with spoken words. Words have power. We need to ask ourselves, "What kind of "power" am I releasing by the words I speak? Are they words of "life" or "death" *Pro18:21,* "encouragement" or "discouragement," etc?

7. Power of Prayer
Ps 5:3; Jer 33:3; Mt 6:6, 7:7, 11; Mk 11:24; Acts 4:31, 12:5; Eph 6:18; Phil 4:6-7; Jms 5:16
Faith and prayer are the channels through which God works to convict, reveal His will, to advance His cause, to protect, perform miracles, energize, and to bless others.

Remember to keep this prayer format in mind:
Fear of the Lord + Faith + Humility + Biblical Thinking (promises) + Obedience + Acknowledgement of God in all your ways + Purity of Heart + Intensity of Desire + Intensity of Prayer + Honoring of Prayer Principles = Results

8. Power of Praise and Thanksgiving
Ps 22:3, 34:1, 100:4; Acts 16:25; Eph 5:19-20; Col 3:16-17; I Thess 5:18
The power of praise was reflected in the lives of Paul and Silas, while in the Philippian jail. After praying, they sang praises unto God. Then a miracle took place. The earth shook, prison doors opened, and their bodies were delivered from prison chains and stocks. The power of praise can silence the devil and activate the power of God. *(Acts 16:14-34; Ps 22:3)*

In *II Chron 20:21-22,* the choir was placed in front of Judah's army to sing thanksgiving and praises to God, resulting in a great victory over Judah's enemy.

9. Power of Jesus' Name
Jn 14:13-14, 15:16; Eph 5:20; Col 3:17; Phil 2:9-11
Jesus' name is above all names. It represents all power within the Universe, especially the Power of the Resurrection. *Eph 1:19-21.* We are to use His name in prayer to rebuke the demonic world and to claim victory and healing for those in need. Pray in Jesus' Name. *Jn 14:13-14,15:16;* Command in Jesus' Name. *Acts 3:6.*

Read *Mt 18:20, 28:18-20; Mk 16:17; Lk 10:17; Jn 14:13; Rom 10:13; Col 3:17; Eph 1:21; Jms 5:14*

10. <u>Power of the Joy of the Lord</u>
Ps 32:11; Neh 8:10; Hab 3:17-18; Jn 15:11; Rom 14:17; Gal 5:22-23; Phil 4:4; II Thess 5:16; I Pt 1:7

The joy of the Lord comes from a personal relationship with Christ, the indwelling of the Holy Spirit, and serving a cause greater than oneself, along with a profound faith in God, and the incorporation of God's Word within our heart and mind. Consequently, we are able to perceive, evaluate, and interpret life's events in the context of God's providence, purposes, and promises, which brings about a profound sense of inner peace and well-being.

This profound sense of peace and well-being:
Motivates
Energizes
Excites, and
Strengthens the spirit until there is an overflow of praise and thanksgiving.

Therefore, we must continually contend for and protect the joy of the Lord within our heart. Always be on guard against the numerous thieves that can interrupt and steal Christian joy.

15 Major Robbers of Christian Joy

-Unresolved anger *Eph 4:26*
-Bitterness/malice because of unforgiveness *Eph 4:31-32*
-Critical/negative spirit *Phil 2:14-15*
-Demanding spirit *Eph 5:21*
-Discontented spirit *Phil 4:11; Heb 13:5*
-Envy and jealousy *I Pt 2:1-2*
-Fearful and worried spirit *II Tim 1:7; Phil 4:6; I Pt 5:7*
-Greedy spirit (covetousness) *Lk 12:15; Heb 13:5; Eph 5:5*
-Hypocritical spirit *I Pt 2:1-2*
-Impatient spirit *Rom 12:12*
-Judgmental spirit *Mt 7:1*
-Negative thinking *Phil 4:8* and spiritual negligence *I Tim 4:14*
-Ungrateful spirit *I Thess 5:18*
-Victim's mentality (poor me, self-pity)
-Works of the flesh and worldliness *Gal 5:16-26; I Jn 2:15-17*

Please take a few moments and evaluate the amount of Christian joy your life reflects both privately and publically. Never forget this spiritual truism, "the greater your spiritual joy, the greater your spiritual power." Can you honestly say, "...*the joy of the Lord is my strength*"? *Neh 8:10*

Conclusion:

The gift of life has been given to us. It is to be lived in a problematic world. But in spite of all the problems we may encounter, it is God's will that we live our life to the fullest, be blessed by Him, seek to transform the world around us, prepare for and keep in perspective our eternal existence, and live triumphantly in Christ.

This abundant and victorious life is revealed throughout scripture. The necessary spiritual resources are provided through God's great plan of redemption—His Son, His Spirit, His Word, His Church.

It is our responsibility to incorporate the essential spiritual virtues by which we were designed for optimal living, and by faith accept God's provision for the "overcoming" life in Christ. If we do so, we can be assured that God will make us to be:

Victors and not victims
Overcomers and not the "over-comed"
Winners and not losers
Strong and not weak
Blessed and not cursed in life
Courageous and not fearful
Delivered and not defeated
Fruitful and not barren

The next time a major problem comes your way, be sure to do the following:

Number 1:
Take time to check on these 7 things about your Christian life.

Faith – Is it strong or is it weak? Are you using your problem to develop your faith?

Attitude – Is it optimistic or pessimistic? Positive or negative? *Phil 4:4; I Thess 5:18; Jms 1:2-4* (Remember, God favors a positive attitude.)

Christian Citizenship – Are you remembering your eternal citizenship? Don't forget our earthly citizenship is only temporary, but our heavenly citizenship is eternal. *Phil 3:20-21*

Thinking – Is it Biblical or secular? Is it magnifying the problem and minimizing the promises? *II Cor 10:5*

Spiritual Standing – Are you standing on the Promises of God, or on the premises of human reasoning?

Opportunity Viewed – for God to work a miracle in your life. *Mt 17:20*

Acknowledgement of God's Power and Providence at work in your life. *Rom 8:28; Phil 1:6*

Number 2:
Take time to reassure yourself of the following five realities about God and your spiritual life.

We have <u>God at work</u> in life's problems to teach us, refine us, and to demonstrate His power through us. *Rom 8:28-29; Jms 1:2-4*

We have <u>God's blessings</u> upon us. Ps 5:12

We have <u>God's protection</u> around us. Isa 54:17; Ps 34:7

We have <u>God's promises</u> for us. II Pt 1:4; Rom 15:4

We have <u>God's power</u> within us. Eph 3:20; I Jn 4:4

Number 3:

Remember the Lord's promises to the overcomers of the 7 churches in the Book of Revelation. (NIV) We by faith can claim these promises for our own spiritual enrichment and personal resolve to be a true overcomer in Christ.

Rev 2:7   *"To him who overcomes, I will give the right to eat from the tree of life, which is in the paradise of God."*

Rev 2:11   *"He who overcomes will not be hurt at all by the second death."*

Rev 2:17   *"To him who overcomes I will give...him a white stone, and a new name written on the stone which no one knows but he who receives it."*

Rev 2:26, 28   *"To him that overcomes and does my will to the end, I will give authority over the nations...I will also give him the morning star."*

Rev 3:5   *"He who overcomes, will like them, be dressed in white. I will never erase his name from the book of life, but will acknowledge his name before my father and his angels."*

Rev 3:12   *"Him who overcomes I will make a pillar in the Temple of my God..."*

Rev 3:21   *"To him who overcomes, I will give the right to sit with me on my throne..."*

May it be our spiritual resolve to live the "abundant life" in Christ. May we so live as to enjoy the multiple blessings of God upon our life. May we have the spiritual discipline, the necessary Christian virtues, and the kind of Biblical faith that will enable us to say, as did the Apostle Paul,
"I have fought a good fight,
I have finished the course (race),
I have kept the faith..." II Tim 4:7

And, wouldn't it be wonderful that all who knew us could say at the end of our earthly journey, "He (She) truly lived the abundantly blessed and victorious life through Christ in this problematic world." *Jn 10:10*

Addendum I
Basic Sinful Forces Within the Sinful and Carnal Heart

Scriptures: Ps 139:23-24; Jer 17:9; Mt 15:18-20

1. Deifying Force - To worship self, others, and things rather than the true and living God. Idolatry is a by-product of this force.

2. Defying Force - To rebel against God, authority, and law. Rebellion.

3. Demanding Force - To assert selfish demands and insist on personal will, way, and rights.

4. Defaming Force - To discredit others through slander, gossip deception, etc.

5. Deceptive Force - To distort truth for personal gain. It is a major defect of the sinful heart. Jer 17:9

6. Disruptive Force - To cause conflict, confusion, and contention which interrupt harmony and peace.

7. Destructive Force - To hurt, attack, destroy, or kill. From this force comes murder, violence, and war.

8. Disrespectful Force - To disregard the feelings, thoughts, rights, boundaries, property and position of others. It leads to abuse and stealing!

9. Envious-Jealous Force - Envy – To resent and desire another's success, status, position, possessions and abilities. Jealous – The fear that what one possesses could be taken by another.

10. Fleshly-Lustful Force - To disregard the spirit of man and succumb to an undisciplined lifestyle that can lead to intemperance and immorality. To be governed by feelings, rather than principles, virtues, or truth.

11. Greedy Force - To covet or crave more and more power, possessions, pleasure, popularity, food, money, etc. Non-benevolent.

12. Hateful Force - To detest, abhor, to be mean, resent, despise

13. Intemperate Force - To lack discipline and moderation

14. Judgment Force - To be judgmental and harshly critical of another without all the facts.

15. Manipulative-Controlling
   Force -   To speak or act in such a way as to unduly influence or
                                  exploit to one's own advantage. Power grabbing.

16. Prideful Force -   To arrogantly promote self above God and others.

17. Revengeful Force -   To strike back – to get even – unforgiving – vindictive.

18. Selfish Anger Force -   To unfairly use anger to manipulate, attack, retaliate, and
                                 destroy. This kind of anger is in some form or fashion
                                 associated with all of the above.

19. Spiritually Skeptical Force -   To doubt, disbelieve, or call into question spiritual realities.

20. Suspicious Force -   To excessively perceive that people always have ulterior
                                 motives and are never to be trusted.

Addendum II
Those Whom God Specifically Blesses

1. Those who avoid vengeance and retaliation. *I Pt 3:9; Rom 12:19*

2. Those who believe by faith and not by sight. *Jn 20:29*

3. Those who care for the poor and needy. *Ps 41:1-2; Pro 22:9; Lk 14:13-14*

4. Those who delight in the Lord and in His law. *Ps 1:1, 37:4*

5. Those who endure trials and temptations. *Jms 1:12*

6. Those who fear the Lord. *Ps 112:1-2, 115:13-14; Pro 22:14, 28:14 (NIV)*

7. Those who give generously. *Deut 15:9-10; Ps 41:1-2, 37:26; Pro 22:9*

8. Those who honor the Lord with their income (substance). *Pro 3:9-10*

9. Those who humble themselves before God. *II Chr 7:14; Pro 22:4; I Pt 5:5-7*

10. Those who listen to the Lord. *Pro 8:34*

11. Those who meditate on the Word of the Lord. *Ps 1:1-3; Josh 1:8*

12. Those who obey the Word of the Lord. *Ex 15:26; Deut 11:26-28; Pro 8:32; Lk 11:28*

13. Those who pray effectively and fervently as a righteous person. *I Pt 3:12; Jms 5:16*

14. Those who have a pure heart. *Ps 24:3-5; Mt 5:8*

15. Those who respect and obey the Lord. *Ps 128:1-2*

16. Those who suffer for righteousness sake. *Mt 5:10-12*

17. Those who tithe. *Mal 3:10; Pro 3:9-10*

18. Those who trust in the Lord. *Jer 17:7; Ps 40:4, 84:4, 12; Pro 16:20*

19. Those who walk in the light of the Lord. *Ps 89:15*

20. Those who wisely seek God's wisdom. *Pro 3:13-18; Jms 1:5*

21. Those who worship the Lord. *Ex 23:25; Ps 84:4*

Addendum III
Spiritual Declarations of My "I Am's" in Christ (Our Identity)

Since Christ is my Lord and Savior, I have the right to begin each day by saying, I Am:

1. Adopted, Accepted, Approved, and Anointed by God, and I am Armed with "can do" power. I am the "Apple of His Eye."

2. Born Again, Blood Washed, Baptized, Bible Believing Christian with a Heavenly Birth Certificate.

3. Blessed by the Almighty God.

4. (The) Child of the Most High God, Crowned with His favor, and I am Confident that "I can do all things through Christ..."

5. (A) Citizen of the Heavenly World.

6. Delivered from Sin's Captivity and Determined to follow Christ.

7. Elevated to a Higher Plain of Life.

8. Empowered by God and Equipped for the battles.

9. Faith driven.

10. Forgiven.

11. Grace Abounded and Surrounded.

12. Heaven Bound.

13. Hopeful of the Second Coming of Christ.

14. Inspired by the Word of God.

15. (An) Inheritor of the Riches of Christ, for I am "an heir and joint heir in Christ."

16. Joyful in the Lord.

17. Justified in the Courts of Heaven.

18. Kept by the Power of God.

19. Loved with an Unconditional Love of God.

20. More than a Conqueror through Christ.

21. (A) New Creature in Christ.

22. I am a Nobody that has become a Somebody within the Nobility of the Universe, for I am a King and a Priest in the Kingdom of Heaven.

23. (An) Overcomer.

24. Peace Maker, Powerful, and a Promise Keeper.

25. Quieted in my Spirit by the Peace of Christ.

26. Redeemed, Regenerated, Resurrected, Renewed in the Spirit of My Mind.

27. Saved and Sanctified.

28. Spirit-filled, Anointed, Led and Directed.

29. (A) Temple of the Most High God.

30. United within the Body of Christ.

31. Victorious.

32. Wearing a Crown of Favor, a Robe of Righteousness, and a Ring of Acceptance and I am walking on the King's Highway.

33. X-ing out the past of which I have no control.

34. Yielded to the Lordship of Christ.

35. Zealous for the Lord.

Addendum IV
Spiritual Declarations of My "I Will's" in Christ (Our Commitments)
(Spiritual Power Thoughts and Songs)

(Remember, *"as he thinketh in his heart (mind) so is he." Pro 23:7*)

As a born-again Christian, you have the right to begin each day by saying:

1. Today, I will have **Abundant** life in Christ. (*Jn 10:10*) *He Abides*

2. Today, I will **Bless** and not curse others. (*Rom 12:14*) *Lord, Make Me a Blessing*

3. Today, I will be **Blessed** by God as I walk humbly before Him, and fear the Lord, and keep His comandments. *(Pro 22:4; Ps 1:1-3)* *Sweeter As the Years Go By*

4. Today, I will **Call** upon the Name of the Lord. *(Jer 33:3). The Lord's Prayer*

5. Today, I will **Cast** all my cares upon the Lord and will not worry. *(I Pt 5:7)*
    What a Friend We Have in Jesus

6. Today, I will and **Can** do all things through Christ who strengthens me. *(Phil 4:13)*
    God Can Do Anything but Fail

7. Today, I will **Delight** myself in the Lord. *(Ps 37:4) Jesus Is All the World to Me*

8. Today, I will be **Determined** to press toward the mark for the prize of the high calling of God in Christ Jesus. *(Phil 3:13-14) I'm Pressing on the Upward Way*

9. Today, I will **Do** unto others as I would have them do unto me. *(Mt 7:12) Do Unto Others*

10. Today, I will be **Emotionally** and Spiritually cleansed from all **emotional** and spiritual garbage—bitterness, wrath, anger, clamor, evil speaking, and malice. *(Eph 4:31) Cleanse Me*

11. Today, I will be **Empowered** by the Spirit of God *(Acts 1:8) O Lord, Send the Power Just Now*

12. Today, I will live and walk by **Faith** and not by fear or worry. *(Rom 1:17; Mt 17:20; Phil 4:6); Faith is the Victory*

13. Today, I will **Fight** the good fight of faith. *(I Tim 6:12) The Fight Is On*

14. Today, I will not live in the spirit of **Fear.** *(II Tim 1:7) Glorious Freedom*

15. Today, I will **Forgive** as I have been forgiven. *(Eph 4:32) I Am Forgiven*

16. Today, I will have all the **Grace** of God I need. *(II Cor 9:8; 12:9) Amazing Grace; Grace That is Greater*

17. Today, I will be **Grateful** for I am blessed. *(I Thess 5:18) Count Your Blessings*

18. Today, I will have **Heart Purity.** *(Ps 24:3-5, 51:10, 139:23-24; Mt 5:8; I Tim 1:5; I Pt 1:22)*

19. Today, I will live in the spirit of **Hope:** The hope that something good is going to happen today in my life *(Rom 15:4; Heb 11:l);* The hope of the Second Coming of the Lord Jesus Christ. *(Titus 2:11-13) Blessed Assurance*

20. Today, I will be **Inspired** by the Word of God. *(Heb 4:12; II Tim 3:16-17) Wonderful Words of Life*

21. Today, I will be **Indwelt** by the Spirit of God. *(Eph 5:18)*

22. Today, I will endeavor to be **Just** in all my relationships and will "love mercy" and walk humbly with God. *(Micah 6:8) Fill My Way Every Day With Love*

23. Today, I will have the **Joy** of the Lord in my heart, which is my strength. *(Neh 8:10) Joy Unspeakable*

24. Today, I will be **Kept** by the power of God through faith. *(I Pt 1:5) I Know Whom I Have Believed*

25. Today, I will be **Loved** by God with an everlasting love. *(Jer 31:3; Jn 3:16) Jesus Loves Me*

26. Today, I will be **More** than a conqueror through Christ. *(Rom 8:31, 35-39) I Will Make the Darkness Light Before You; Victory in Jesus*

27. Today, I will be a **Mountain Mover** by faith. *(Mt 17:20). God Specializes In Things Thought Impossible*

28. Today, I will **Not be a Nobody**, but I will be a somebody within the nobility of God's universe. *(I Pt 2:9; Col 3:12; Rev.1:6) I'm a Child of the King*

29. Today, I will be an **Overcomer** of all my adversities, battles, circumstances, and the world through Christ. *(I Jn 5:4) Faith is the Victory*

30. Today, I will be a **Peace Maker** and not a trouble maker. *(Mt 5:8; Rom 12:18) Let There Be Peace On Earth*

31. Today, I will be a **Positive** person, thinking **Positive** thoughts, and speaking **Positive** words. *(Phil 4:4,8) Wonderful Words of Life*

32. Today, I will **Praise** and bless the Lord. *(Ps 34:1, 103:1-2) Doxology*

33. Today, I will fulfill the **Purpose** for which God designed me. *(Jere 29:11) Take My Life and Let It Be*

34. Today, I will not be a **Quitter.** *(Phil 3:13-14) We're Marching to Zion*

35. Today, I will be **Quieted** in the storms of life by the Prince of Peace. *(Jn 14:27, 16:33)* *'Til the Storm Passes Over*

36. Today, I will **Rejoice i**n the Lord. *(Phil 4:4) Again, I Say Rejoice*

37. Today, I will **Rest** in the Lord. *(Mt 11:28) The Haven of Rest*

38. Today, I will **Resist** the devil, the world, and the flesh. *(Jms 4:7; Rom 8:1-5, 12:2; Gal 5:13-26) Turn Your Eyes Upon Jesus*

39. Today, I will **Speak** words of Faith, Affirmation, Inspiration, Thanksgiving, Hope, Optimism, Praise, Expectancy. *(Ps 19:14, 39:1) Let the Words of My Mouth; O, For a Thousand Tongues*

40. Today, I will be **Spirit** filled, **Spirit** empowered, and **Spirit** led. *(Rom 8:26-27; Gal 5:24-26) Come, Holy Spirit I Need Thee*

41. Today, I will **Stand** on the Promises of God. *(I Pt 1:4) Standing on the Promises*

42. Today, I will be **Teachable** in my spirit. *(II Tim 2:15) Take My Life and Let It Be*

43. Today, I will be **Thankful** in everything. *(I Thess 5:18) Count Your Blessings*

44. Today, I will **Trust** in the Lord with all my heart. *(Pro 3:5) Trust and Obey*

45. Today, I will be a **Uniter** and not a divider among God's people. *(Phil 2:2-3) The Family of God*

46. *Today,* I will be a **Victor** and not a Victim, a Winner and not a Whiner, all because of God's promises and power. *(Isa 54:17; Rom 8:31, 35-38) Victory in Jesus*

47. Today, I will **Walk** by faith and not by sight and will do God's Will here on earth as it is in Heaven. *(II Cor 5:7; Gen 5:21-24; Mt 6:9-10) Oh, I Love to Walk With Jesus*

48. Today, I will **X-out** all of my past of which I have no control *(Phil 3:13-14)*, and my todays and tomorrows will be better than my yesterdays. *Calvary Covers It All*

49. Today, I will **Yield** all of my spirit, soul, and body to the Lordship of Christ. *(I Thess 5:23) I Surrender All*

50. Today, I will have the **Zeal** of the Lord upon me, and around me, and within me, and will be filled with the zip, zap, and zest of the Spirit. *(II Kings 19:31; Isa 9:7, 37:32, 42:13, 59:17; Acts 1:8; Rom 12:11) The Joy of the Lord is My Strength*

Addendum V
Spiritual Declarations of My "I Will Not's" in Christ (Our Resolve)

By the Grace of God "I Will Not":

1. Abandon the Faith or Align myself with the Devil, World, or the Flesh.

2. Backslide or Backbite.

3. Curse, but rather Bless with my tongue.

4. Deceive or Defame others, or Doubt God.

5. Envy.

6. Fear but trust in God.

7. Find Fault, or Forget what God has done for me and my family.

8. Give up, Give in or Cave in.

9. Grieve the Holy Spirit.

10. Hinder the Holy Spirit.

11. Injure others knowingly.

12. (Be) Judgmental.

13. Keep grudges or seek revenge.

14. Look down, Look back, but rather Look Up.

15. Murmur or Complain.

16. Neglect my Holy Habits—Prayer, Bible Reading, Worship.

17. Obey the devil, world, or the flesh.

18. Overlook God's Providence in my life, but rather "acknowledge Him in all my ways."

19. Pessimistically view life.

20. Play Games with God, but rather endeavor to be the "Real Deal."

21. Quench the Spirit.

22. Resist the Spirit.

23. Seek my will but rather God's Will.

24. Speak ill of others.

25. Think negatively, but rather Biblically.

26. Unite myself with the world or the things of the world.

27. (Be) Vindictive in spirit.

28. Worry.

29. X-out what God has done for me and my family.

30. Yield to temptation, the devil, the world, or the flesh.

31. (Lack) Zeal for the Lord, His Church, and His Word.

Bibliography

Chapter 1

Warren, Rick. *The Purpose Driven Life.* Zondervan Publishing House, 2002.

Chapter 2

Wesley, John. *A Plain Account of Christian Perfection*, 1777

Chapter 3

Campbell, Don, Johnston, Wendell, Walvoord, John and Witmer, John. *The Theological Wordbook.* Word Publishing, Inc., 2000

Gruden, Wayne. *Systematic Theology.* Inter-Varsity Press and Zondervan Publishing House, 1994.

Unger, Merrill F. and White, William. *Nelson's Expository of the Old Testament.* Thomas Nelson Publishers, Nashville, 1980.

Unger, Merrill F. *Unger's Bible Dictionary.* Moody Press, 1951.

Vine, W.E. *Vine's Complete Expository Dictionary.* Thomas Nelson Publishers, 1984.

Wiley, H. Orton. *Christian Theology*, *Vol III.* Beacon Hill Press, 1952.

Chapter 4

Metz, Donald S. *Studies in Biblical Holiness.* Beacon Hill Press, 1971.

Purkiser, W.T. *Sanctification and It's Synonyms.* Beacon Hill Press, 1961.

Chapter 5

Earle, Ralph, Blaney, Harvey and Hanson. *Exploring the New Testament.* Beacon Hill Press, 1955. pp 260-369, 405-409

Willmington, Harold L. *Willmington's Bible Handbook.* Tyndale House Publishers, Inc., 1997. pp 661-776.

Chapter 6

Murphy, Ed. *Spiritual Warfare.* Thomas Nelson Publishers, 1992.

Made in the USA
Coppell, TX
16 January 2024

27750338R00057